THE UNIVERSE WANTS TO PLAY
THE ANOMALIST 12: A NONFICTION ANTHOLOGY

EDITED BY PATRICK HUYGHE
AND DENNIS STACY

Anomalist Books
San Antonio * New York

An Original Publication of ANOMALIST BOOKS

The Universe Wants to Play: The Anomalist 12
Copyright © 2006 by Patrick Huyghe and Dennis Stacy
The authors own the copyright to their individual pieces.
ISBN: 1933665149

"A Heretic For Our Times: A Visit with Rupert Sheldrake" by Jay Walljasper
first appeared in *Ode* magazine(Volume 3, Number 9, November 2005), and
is reprinted with permission.

Cover image: NASA/JPL/Space Science Institute. Image taken by the Cassini-
Huygens orbiter of Saturn's pale, icy moon Dione, with golden hued Saturn in
the distance, and a couple of the planet's magnificent rings viewed as horizontal
stripes near the bottom of the image.

Book design by Ansen Seale

Anomalist Books   Anomalist Books
5150 Broadway #108   PO Box 577
San Antonio, TX 78209   Jefferson Valley, NY 10535

CONTENTS

The Universe wants to play.
– Hakim Bey

COMMENTARY:
BELIEF IN BELIEF
By Joseph M. Felser, Ph.D.

If Stavrogin believes, he does not think he believes.
If he does not believe, he does not think he does not believe.
– The Possessed

"Do you think that scientific proof of life after death would change the world for the better?" asks a veteran paranormalist in a recent volume.[1] For the venerable author, it is clear that this question is strictly rhetorical. We are to assume that what philosophers have traditionally called "knowledge," or Justified True Belief—JTB for short—matters. But does it? Is JTB the anomalist's Holy Grail? Or, is it strictly a red herring?

I hate to be the skunk at the garden party (and some of my best friends are—or were—parapsychologists), but I have come to the conclusion that it is utterly pointless to attempt to prove the reality of the paranormal scientifically. This may come as a shock, but proof is part of the problem, not the solution. What we need is nothing less than an epistemological exorcism to banish that old devil, belief. We are possessed by an idea.

Faith in abstract propositions goes back at least 2500 years, to the Greeks. According to the classical scholar Peter Kingsley,[2] it was Socrates and Plato who transformed the experiential search for wisdom, as practiced by shaman-seers like Parmenides, into a purely intellectualized, second-order discourse about the search for wisdom. The goal was to obtain universal definitions of concepts (e.g., "piety," "justice") that would apply to anyone and everyone, in all times and places, regardless of their personal experience or actual circumstances. Previously concerned with the articulation of inspired visions, philosophy became obsessed with winning conviction by argument. Everybody had to get on board. Opponents were to be bludgeoned into submission with the heavy club of logic. Clever talk (and lots of it) replaced the vision quest as the *sine qua non* of philosophical inquiry as belief moved to center stage.

This pivotal position was cemented five hundred years later with the creation of a new religion. When St. Paul decided to market Christianity to the unwashed masses, he wisely jettisoned the onerous Judaic emphasis on ritual practice and ignored the ostensibly élitist Gnostic ideal of inward experience. Instead, Paul astutely made sheer belief, in Walter Kaufmann's memorable phrase, the one and only "gate to salvation."[3] Beliefs acquired a kind of magical power. It's not what you did or what you experienced that counted, but simply what you believed. This mantra would be repeated over and again in subsequent Christian history, from Martin Luther's dictum, "Faith, not works," to President Eisenhower's ecumenical benediction that everyone should have some religious belief "and I don't care what it is." Such is the sad secularized apotheosis of what philosopher Alasdair MacIntyre once dubbed "the belief in belief."[4]

But what must be borne in mind is that Bacon's famous (or infamous) equation, "Knowledge is power," also fits squarely within this tradition. For all its vaunted empiricism, modern science inherited the concept of natural law from biblical monotheism and, with it, the Christian fetish of belief. (As Jung understood, all westerners are reflexively Christian in their habits of thought.) Thus Galileo was right, the Inquisition that condemned him wrong. So what? There was no real revolution here. We merely had two True Believers squaring off against each other. One blinked, getting his revenge only posthumously. Today all educated people profess to believe that the earth goes around the sun, and not vice-versa. But is anything really changed by this profession? Our ordinary language robustly refuses to be badgered into submission. We still speak, without apparent guilt or embarrassment, of "sunrise" and "sunset." Many philosophers will mutter in disgust, "So much the worse for ordinary language." Yet, embedded in this stubborn refusal to be cowed by an abstraction is a fundamentally healthy reflex at work. Science, like its predecessor Christianity, uses its social prestige and power to enforce compliance and root out dissent.[5] Ordinary language may be the last refuge of the independent minded true empiricist.

When paranormalists hungry for validation by the scientific priesthood agree to play the old "Prove it to the Skeptic" and "Torture the Secrets out of Mother Nature" game, they are unknowingly worshipping at the bloody altar of belief in belief. However, I have a nagging suspicion that what the maverick paranormalist Rhea A. White dubs "Exceptional Human Experiences" (or EHEs) neither ask for nor require belief of this kind. Rather, as White has suggested,[6] EHEs call us to enact a different, less invasive and controlling, relationship to our world. In the process, we are forced to learn to pay attention to what we actually experience, as opposed to what we think we ought to experience. When and if we do this, the paranormal will cease to be "para." It will become a normal part of our world and our natural way of perceiving it. No one will have to convince anyone of anything.

In a way, this is nothing new. "'Primitive' thinkers," argued the late, great iconoclast Paul Feyerabend, "showed greater insight into the nature of knowledge than their 'enlightened' philosophical rivals."[7] Perhaps this is why those few dissident holdovers from "primitive" cultures often react with barely controlled hilarity at the contorted epistemological gyrations of the average Western paranormalist. Phenomena that, to us, are amazing, unusual, or unbelievable are, as the Abenaki writer Joseph Bruchac wryly observes, "as everyday as eating and sleeping" to the indigenous inhabitants of the Americas.[8] "Within the tribal setting," notes the Sioux philosopher Vine Deloria, "revelation is not regarded as an unusual situation."[9] Why is this? Why are we Westerners so blind to the obvious?

As Deloria acknowledges, for the Western mind belief almost always trumps actual experience.[10] He describes, for example, how present-day astronomers are scouring the records of non-western societies (including those of the North American Indians) for evidence of a celestial supernova that occurred in 1054. Few medieval Europeans witnessed this event because they did not believe it could happen. They held that since a perfect God made the heavens, He made them perfectly stable and uniform. Comets, supernovas, and meteors need not apply. These catastrophic intrusions did not fit in with the medieval conception of a divinely appointed order. As a result, people literally did not see what they were seeing.

Deloria attributes the native insistence on the fidelity to the particular details and epistemological priority of concrete experience over ideology to the Indians' bond with specific features of the natural landscape.[11] The Indian is concerned, not with putatively universal laws of nature, but with this tree, this lake, this mountain, and the experiences they engender. Particular places and objects are "holy" (*wakan*), meaning that they are power points where the mysterious energies of the universe coalesce. However, because all things are connected in a living tapestry, these nodal points would not exist if everything else were not also in its proper place. Thus Deloria cites with approval Claude Lévi Strauss's observation: "A native thinker makes the penetrating comment that 'all sacred things must have their place' . . . . It could even be said that being in their place is what makes them sacred, for if they were taken out of their place, even in thought, the entire order of the universe would be destroyed. Sacred objects therefore contribute to the maintenance of order in the universe by occupying the places allocated to them."[12]

From the standpoint of a sacred geography, then, nothing is superfluous and nothing is dispensable. Everything is as it should be. This recognition simultaneously shatters another pillar of the Western belief in belief: the ideology of progress. From its inception, the belief in belief has been wedded to one form or another of the grand illusion: every day, in every way (spiritual, material, or cognitive), things are supposed to be getting better and better. The Truth (or Heaven, or the Big Score) is always Out There, somewhere else, off in the future. The expectation that "scientific proof of life after death would change the world for the better" is symptomatic of this tenacious ailment.

Is there a cure? What would happen if the perennially anxious Western mind, with its desperate drive to prove and improve, broke through to the experiential perspective of so-called "primitives"? How might this transform our approach to the paranormal?

Happily, I can here turn from the miasma of armchair academic speculation to the bracing tonic of direct observation.

Several years ago I had a student I'll call Mike in one of my philosophy classes. Mike was a puzzle. A recent immigrant from Ukraine, he spoke a heavily accented English. Quiet and unassuming, with his spiky blonde haircut and perpetual smile, Mike radiated good will and a kind of calm cheerfulness that I did not ordinarily associate with anyone of his youthful age. He had that indefinable sense of presence we call "authority." Whenever I would get too preachy in my remarks, Mike would calmly insist that the world didn't need to be reformed. I would feel chastened. I couldn't figure him out.

One day after class, Mike confessed to me that he wanted to become a filmmaker. He longed to communicate something that he felt was ultimately incommunicable. Yet he wanted to try anyway. He alluded cryptically to an experience he had had back in Odessa. I did not pry, and he was not yet ready to discuss it. Some months later, knowing of my interest in unusual experiences, Mike explained what had happened to him.

It seems that one night, Mike inhaled a bit too much of Mother Nature. What Mother Nature then revealed to him was astonishing. As his thoughts raced "with an incredible speed," he was suddenly filled with a mystical knowledge of all things. "I understood all the laws of nature," said Mike, "all the physics, math, geology—I knew EVERYTHING. All of a sudden everything made perfect sense." At the same time, he felt deeply connected with all things; so much so that, "If I'd wanted to I could have destroyed the world just by moving my finger and breaking the order of something that made it all alive. But I couldn't. Not physically, not mentally."

What is so striking about this description is that it exactly parallels Lévi Strauss's remark that, for the indigenous mind, the removal of sacred things from their rightful place, even in thought, would bring about the destruction of the entire order of the universe. What Mike brought back from his exhilarating thrill ride into an expanded awareness was not an abstract knowledge of theories and principles, but an immediate feeling of connection with a living, conscious, intelligent universe in which everything is already in its proper place. It is no wonder, then, that he instinctively resisted all my edifying blather. The script from which Mike read is an old one indeed; one that pre-Socratics like Parmenides— not to mention Black Elk—would have recognized.

But was this a genuine breakthrough, or rather a breakdown—a psychological regression to an archaic level of mind best left to lowly "primitives"? During his episode, Mike said that the tendrils of his awareness expanded to include his parents on the other side of the city and his friends in the next building. He could see them and hear their conversations. And when he later told them what they had said, this was confirmed.

Of course, such "merely anecdotal" evidence would not count as scientific proof of the validity of Mike's experience. He could care less. The definitive Answers for which the rest of us anxiously seek are of no interest to those who are comfortable with the unanswerable questions posed by the mystery of existence. What we call anomalies draw us into a direct experience of this great mystery, against which the standardized beliefs, creeds, and formulas of the "civilized" mind are meant to serve as a comfortable buffer. The time has come to throw away the security blanket and invite reality in. The only things we have to lose are our illusions. Let the beliefs fall where they may.

NOTES

1 Susy Smith, *The Afterlife Codes: Searching for Evidence of the Survival of the Soul.* (Charlottesville, VA: Hampton Roads, 2000), 213.
2 Peter Kingsley, *In the Dark Places of Wisdom.* (Inverness, CA: The Golden Sufi Center, 1999).
3 Walter Kaufmann, *Critique of Religion and Philosophy.* (Princeton, NJ: Princeton University Press, 1978), 294.
4 See his essay, *"The Fate of Theism,"* in Alasdair MacIntyre and Paul Ricoeur, The Religious Significance of Atheism (New York: Columbia University Press, 1970), 21.
5 See Paul Feyerabend, *Against Method* (London: NLB, 1975).
6 White began her career over forty years ago as a disciple of J.B. Rhine, the father of modern experimental parapsychology. But in the last decade her work has taken a very different tack. See, for example, her essays "An Experience-Centered Approach to Parapsychology" and "Seek Ye First the Kingsom of Heaven: What are EHEs and What Can We Do About Them?" in *Exceptional Human Experience, Vol. 11, No. 2* (December

1993).

7 Feyerabend, *Against Method*, 298.

8 From the introduction to his novel, *The Waters Between* (Hanover, NH: 1998), xiv-xv.

9 Vine Deloria, *For This Land: Writings on Religion in America* (New York: Routledge, 1999), 157.

10 Vine Deloria, *God is Red: A Native View of Religion*, 2nd ed. (Golden, CO: Fulcrum, 1994), 136.

11 See, for example, the chapter on "Thinking in Time and Space" in *God is Red* and also the essay on "Tribal Religious Realities," in *Spirit and Reason: The Vine Deloria, Jr. Reader* (Golden, CO: Fulcrum, 1999).

12 Cited in Deloria, *Spirit and Reason*, 362.

JOSEPH M. FELSER, Ph.D. graduated Summa Cum Laude and Phi Beta Kappa from Boston University, and received his doctorate from the University of Chicago. He is currently Associate Professor of Philosophy at Kingsborough Community College of the City University of New York. Felser is the author of over 30 published articles on religion, myth, philosophy, parapsychology, and the paranormal. His first book, *The Way Back to Paradise: Restoring the Balance between Magic and Reason (2005)*, was published by Hampton Roads.

A HERETIC FOR OUR TIMES:
A VISIT WITH RUPERT SHELDRAKE
By Jay Walljasper

Walking to the home of maverick scientist Rupert Sheldrake in Hampstead – London's cozy but glamorous artistic village that's been home to John Keats, George Orwell, D.H. Lawrence and, more recently, novelist John LeCarre and actress Emma Thompson – I am not surprised to find that his plain brick house looks out on Hampstead Heath. This famous (and still remarkably wild) expanse of grasslands and groves was the spot where Keats met William Wordsworth for long rambles, discussing the passions and ideas that would be immortalized in their Romantic poetry. Sheldrake, one of the world's leading spokesmen for a more holistic and democratic vision of science, might easily be grouped with the Romantics, except that his insights about the world are based on empirical research rather than poetic feelings.

Sheldrake's bold theories about how the universe works sparked controversy in 1981 with the publication of *A New Science of Life*. Actually it wasn't the book itself that brought Sheldrake's ideas to prominence but an incendiary editorial by the editor of the respected British journal *Nature*, Sir John Maddox, who fumed, "This infuriating tract... is the best candidate for burning there has been for many years." That was quite a lot of attention for a young scientist, especially one who at that time was working as a plant physiologist in India.

What so infuriated Maddox was Sheldrake's theory of "morphic resonance" – a complicated framework of ideas proposing that nature relies upon its own set of memories, which are transmitted through time and space via "morphic fields." [See "Morphic Resonance 101."] The theory holds that these fields, which operate much like electrical or magnetic fields, shape our entire world. A panda bear is a panda bear because it naturally tunes into morphic fields containing

The Making of a Maverick Scientist

Rupert Sheldrake knew early on he wouldn't fit in as a conventional scientist. He had been drawn to biology because of his love of animals, but after enrolling at Cambridge he discovered that in "studying biology you mostly killed animals for experiments." Earning his Ph.D. in 1966, Sheldrake was made a Fellow at Cambridge's Clare College and a Fellow of the Royal Society. A bright career in biochemistry awaited him, but his mind was swirling with ideas outside the boundaries of science-as-usual. He just couldn't accept the view of his colleagues that the universe functioned like piece of machinery when much of what he was thinking, reading, feeling, and increasingly finding in his research told him it was more like a living, breathing creature.

"I think the whole culture is split on this," he says. "Most people go along with the 9 to 5 Monday through Friday mechanistic worldview because that's what the economy is based upon. But on the weekends a lot of them go out in the country, or sit in their garden or play with their pets. Then they easily accept that the universe is a living thing."

This seems to describe the life Sheldrake was leading at Cambridge. But one evening in 1973, he was out walking in the gardens of Clare College when a huge idea struck him: What if there were memory fields, like magnetic or electrical fields, that were capable of transmitting information across time? It sounded crazy, but so would the idea of television images being transmitted through the airwaves have if you had been talking about it in 1890. He called his theory *morphic resonance*. "The idea didn't get much of a reception in the biochemistry department," he remembers. "They really couldn't see the point of it. But I saw this as a paradigm shift. I knew right away it would be my long-term project. I also knew these views would be treated as deeply heretical."

The next year he took a job at the International Crops Research Institute for the Semi-Arid Tropics near Hyderabad, strongly drawn to India as a place where he could more comfortably think about the universe in new ways. While conducting experiments with chickpeas and pigeonpeas by day, he was also mapping out the possibilities of morphic resonance and studying Hindu, Buddhist and Sufi philosophy.

"But I realized that no matter how hard I tried I couldn't become a Hindu," he confesses. "I found myself being drawn back to Christianity." When it finally came time to lay out his scientific theories in a book, he took a leave from the Crop Institute and moved into an ashram in South India run by English Benedictine priest Bede Griffiths. Famous for bringing Eastern and Western spiritual traditions under one roof, Griffiths greatly influenced Sheldrake, who in a similar way is building a bridge between the empirical rigor of the West and the holistic perspective of the East.

storehouses of information that define and govern panda bears. The same with pigeons, platinum atoms, and the oak trees on Hampstead Heath, not to mention human beings. This theory, if widely accepted, would turn our understanding of the universe inside out – which is why Sheldrake has so often felt the wrath of orthodox scientists.

For the past 20 years, he has pursued further research on morphic fields even though no university or scientific institute would dare hire him. Much of his empirical explorations focus on unsolved phenomena such as how pigeons and other animals find

Morphic Resonance 101

The essence of Rupert Sheldrake's morphic resonance theory is that genes alone cannot explain how plants and animals –indeed, life itself – develop. While that sounds radical to our ears, it is not a totally new idea. Around 1920 three prominent biologists – Hans Spemann, Alexander Gurwitsch and Paul Weiss – each independently concluded that some kind of field plays a role in making sure that a sunflower turns out to become the tall flower with bright yellow petals that we recognize rather than, say, a petunia or a penguin.

Sheldrake's work takes their concept one step further by offering an explanation for how these "morphic fields" might work. "I propose that they are transmitted from past members of the species through a kind of non-local resonance, called morphic resonance," he explains on his website. He suggests that living things are shaped by a sense of memory that does not reside solely in the genes but rather is sent through invisible morphic fields the same way your voice travels via electromagnetic waves when using a mobile phone.

Morphic resonance may help solve some of the mysteries that have intrigued leading scientists through the years. Charles Darwin probed the well-documented phenomenon of "atavism" – in which features of extinct species appear again in other species. Atavism might be explained as living species tapping into the morphic memories of a long-gone species. Ivan Pavlov, the famous Russian physiologist, was baffled by the results of experiments where he trained mice to run to food when an electric bell sounded. It took the first generation an average of 300 trials to learn, but when he switched to a different group of mice, unrelated to the first, they learned much faster. They had a head start, Sheldrake explained to *Discover* magazine. "Subsequent mice would be influenced by morphic resonance from those in the first experiment."

The implications of morphic resonance are staggering, opening up among other things a new way to think about evolution. "Science has this mixed view of evolution right now," Sheldrake says. "Accepting it, but also hanging on to the old clockwork view of the universe as one where things are all fixed. Morphic resonance would mean that all of nature, including its laws, are evolving. It means a shift from the idea that the universe is mechanistic to one that it's really an organism."

their way home from great distances, why people experience feelings in amputated limbs, why some people and animals can sense that someone is staring at them. He believes morphic resonance may offer answers to these questions.

His experimentation has been underwritten by freethinking funders like the late Laurence Rockefeller and the Institute of Noetic Sciences, founded by Apollo astronaut Edgar Mitchell. Through the years Sheldrake has supported his family largely through lecture tours, which draw curious crowds around the world, and a series of books exploring various aspects of what is often called "New Science." He's written on ecological, spiritual, and philosophical themes, as well as a manifesto on how science could be democratized (*Seven Experiments that Could Change the World*) and a bestseller on animal behavior (*Dogs that Know When Their Owners are Coming Home*). His current research involves thousands of rigorously empirical tests probing the existence of telepathy. John Maddox nonetheless has continued to accuse him of "heresy," saying he should be "condemned in exactly the same language that the Pope used to condemn Galileo."

●●●

When Sheldrake answers the door, I find a tall, surprisingly youthful man in a golf shirt and Birkenstock sandals with socks who hardly seems a menacing troublemaker out to destroy civilization as we know it. He welcomes me into his home, which wonderfully fits my expectations of what a slightly bohemian biologist's house should look like: shells, antlers, giant pine cones, fossils and exotic-looking houseplants on display in comfy rooms also filled with books, art, musical instruments, oriental carpets and a few patches of peeling paint. Upstairs is his office, which overflows with scientific journals and papers, and a spacious library room crammed with books on every conceivable subject. A corner of the library houses a small laboratory, which was recently commandeered by his teenage sons as a computer center.

It's a gorgeous sunny morning and Sheldrake suggests we sit in the backyard, which looks to me like a mini-botanical garden. It turns out that I am visiting on a rather momentous occasion. His three-year appointment to a research post at Trinity College in Cambridge will be announced today. It marks a homecoming of sorts to the place where he studied as an undergraduate, earned a Ph.D. and was named a Fellow of Clare College, where he served as Director of Studies in Biochemistry and Cell Biology. [See "The Making of a Maverick Scientist."]

I ask if his appointment signals a growing tolerance of outspoken ideas in science. Not quite, he explains. It's a unique endowment created in the memory of Fredric Myers, a Fellow of Trinity College who was fascinated by psychic phenomena although today it is generally awarded to researchers out to debunk the existence of such phenomena. "But it does mean I will be getting a salary for the first time in 25 years and money to do my research," he says with a sincere grin. "But in the field of biology the holistic approach I advocate is more remote than ever. Funding drives most research toward biotech projects."

"Science is the last unreformed institution in the modern world today," he adds in a matter-of-fact rather than harsh tone. "It's like the church before the Reformation. All decisions are made by a small, powerful group of people. They're authoritarian, entrenched, well-funded and see themselves as a priesthood."

Sheldrake's views are widely shared by many people – indeed by so many that it's seen as a looming problem in Britain and Europe as the public increasingly looks upon science as a tool of corporations and big government, not an institution that benefits average citizens. Kids seem less inclined to pursue careers in the field and taxpayers are growing reluctant about financing research.

"If science were more responsive to democratic input, this would look different," he says. He points out that popular programs on television dealing with scientific themes focus primarily on four topics that interest people: 1) alternative medicine; 2) ecological issues; 3) animals; and 4) parapsychology. But very little scientific funding goes toward research in these areas. He wonders what would happen if people could participate in choosing the kind of research they fund with their tax money.

That's the idea behind Sheldrake's recent proposal to let the public vote on how to spend one percent of the overall science budget – an idea greeted with even more horror than morphic resonance in some scientific circles. But other scientists are giving it serious consideration as a way to win back the public's trust.

More than a symbolic gesture, this would actually add up to quite a sum of money to initiate interesting new research that the scientific establishment won't sanction. Sheldrake notes that independent scientists, including Charles Darwin, have been responsible for many important breakthroughs because they probe for answers in ways quite different than their well-funded peers in universities, research institutes, or corporations. But looking around Britain today the only other independent scientific researcher Sheldrake can think of is James Lovelock, who conceived the revolutionary Gaia hypothesis, which posits that the earth is a living organism.

Public participation is essential to Sheldrake's own research because otherwise he couldn't afford to do it. Right now he's enlisting people worldwide to study email telepathy (the ability to know who's emailing before you get a message). His website (www.sheldrake. org) offers all the details necessary to conduct your own telepathy experiments and to report the findings.

Eighty percent of the population reports experiences with telephone telepathy (email telepathy's older cousin), he explains. In the controlled experiments he's conducted, in which subjects choose which of four close friends is phoning, they're right 42 percent of the time – significantly higher than the 25 percent that would occur by random chance.

"I think we all have a capacity for telepathy," Sheldrake notes. "But it is really a function of close social bonds. It doesn't happen with total strangers. At least not in an experimental setting. And of course some people have a better sense of telepathy than others, just the same as with the sense of smell." He hopes the on-line experiments can identify individuals with particularly strong telepathic skills, who can then be studied further.

"What I am interested in are the mysteries of everyday life – a lot of these simple things are not being investigated," Sheldrake says staring up at the sunny sky with that "lost-in-thought" look you typically associate with scientists. A few moments later he pulls his attention back in my direction, smiles apologetically and continues."I prefer to explore things that people know in their lives or the lives of their friends. I am interested in science that is rooted in people's experience. Indeed, the word empirical means experience."

●●●

By now the two of us have been talking in his garden for several hours and Sheldrake picks up a garden hose to water several tall, exotic-looking plants. I meanwhile silently marvel at the tenacity he's shown in keeping his research going all these years and the gentle spirit he possesses in the face of hostility toward his work. John Maddox has said he practices "magic instead of science" yet Sheldrake brings up Maddox with almost-fondness perhaps because the scathing editorial in *Nature* turned *The New Science of Life* into a bestseller and launched Sheldrake's career as an independent scientist.

It's time for me to go, and a taxi is honking in front of the house to take me to Paddington Station, but I must squeeze in one more question. "How do you refresh yourself, renew your creativity and stay calm in the face of so much criticism?" Sensing my anxiety about missing the train, he efficiently ticks off three answers in the methodical manner you'd expect from a former science whiz kid. "One. Playing the piano, usually Bach. Two. Meditating. Three. Taking walks, usually out on the Heath."

After a hearty handshake I jump into to the cab and, watching Hampstead Heath disappear through the back window, decide that I sold Rupert Sheldrake short earlier today. Comparing him to fellow Heath hikers Keats and Wordsworth, I viewed Sheldrake as a cool and rational man of science while they were warm and passionate poets. But I can see now that even as a dedicated scientist, Sheldrake possesses a poetic imagination in how he thinks about the world and how he lives his life.

JAY WALLJASPER is the executive editor of *Ode*, an international news magazine. This article appeared in *Ode* Volume 3, Number 9, November 2005, and is reprinted with permission. For more information on the magazine see: www.odemagazine.com.

SEX, SERIAL KILLERS, AND ESP
By Michael Schmicker

It sounds like an urban legend, like the alligator living in the city sewer. A woman about to go out on a date with a nicely dressed man suddenly senses something horribly evil about him, cancels the date, and later discovers the man was a homicidal killer.

Could it be more than just a legend? Possibly.

The Rhine Research Center's collection of over 14,000 spontaneous ESP experiences – the largest database of spontaneous ESP reports in the world – contains a small number of reports from women who believe ESP helped them avoid sexual predators intent on inflicting everything from date rape to murder.

In 2005, the Center received a dramatic story involving a teenage girl in eastern Connecticut who reported using ESP to avoid a date with notorious serial killer Michael B. Ross (executed May 2005 by the State of Connecticut). The report was emailed to me by her uncle Bob, a friend of mine who owns a technology consulting company in Mystic, Connecticut. Bob knew Dr. Sally Rhine Feather and I were working on a new book called *The Gift*, which featured spontaneous ESP experiences, and he thought we would find it interesting.

> A number of years ago when my niece Cynthia was living with her parents as a fifteen year-old teenager, she hitchhiked a car ride home from a young man in his twenties.
>
> During the ride, they exchanged pleasantries and the man, named Michael, revealed that he was in the insurance business. Michael asked Cynthia for a dinner date and she accepted.
>
> When she told her parents an insurance man had asked her for a date, even though they didn't want

her to go out with boys until age sixteen, they were delighted. Her mom had been anxious about the caliber of people that Cynthia chose to associate with. It was a typical concern that moms often have for teenage daughters, especially those who are as attractive and well developed as Cynthia was at this age. Her mom had seen Cynthia dropped off before by longhaired, tough guys on motorcycles, known for late nights and drinking. Getting a date with a guy who wore a suit and tie was a very welcome sign.

When Michael arrived for the date, he was met by Cynthia's mother and father and was escorted into the living room to wait for Cynthia to finish getting ready. The parents were very impressed with Michael and were trying their best to make a good impression on him.

When Cynthia finally joined everyone, before she could utter a word, her eye caught Michael's eye. She immediately retreated to her bedroom. Her confused parents tried to smooth over the social infraction, writing it off to the immature behavior of a teenager.

After an uncomfortable ten minutes, her dad went to find Cynthia in her bedroom and encourage her to speed it up, as it was starting to get embarrassing. Cynthia said she was not going anywhere with Michael. She told her father there was something wrong with Michael, and she would not be with him alone. Her father pleaded with her, pressuring her to fulfill her commitment to the date. He finally demanded that she come out and tell her date directly.

Cynthia composed herself and approached Michael with extended hand. She told him frankly that, while he was probably a very nice guy, she was sorry but there was something about him that made her very uncomfortable, and she didn't want to go alone with him. Michael left and never returned.

Cynthia, who never locked or even closed her

bedroom door before, locked the door and windows that night. Several years later Michael was on the front page of all the Connecticut papers. He was Michael Ross, the serial killer who murdered six young women in eastern Connecticut before he was caught.

It's a dramatic story, but it remains just that.

In the first chapter of *The Gift*, we remind readers that the stories we present in the book are not scientific proof for ESP. Proof can only be established in the laboratory, using repeatable experiments. Stories like Cynthia's simply offer us food for thought – anecdotal evidence typically incomplete and heavily dependent on the honesty and the memory of the experiencer.

The Rhine Research Center does a certain amount of screening on stories it receives. Dr. Feather, a licensed clinical psychologist, reviews the letters and emails and accepts reports which in her judgment were submitted in good faith by an apparently sane, mentally balanced individual; include specific details; and which appear to involve information beyond what the normal five senses could provide. She may do a brief follow-up on the more promising cases, posing a few additional questions. But she doesn't play Sherlock Holmes.

She views the stories the same way her mother, Dr. Louisa Rhine, did when she first started collecting ESP accounts. "My mother's work with spontaneous ESP experiences didn't focus on scientific proof," Sally explains. "By 1948, proof of ESP had already been established in the laboratory. My mother collected this anecdotal evidence for a different purpose, knowing that controlled laboratory experiments can impose artificial constraints on the reality they try to analyze. For her, the primary scientific value of such a collection of reports lay in the clues the raw reports provided about patterns of ESP experiences. These patterns could provide valuable new hypotheses to test in the laboratory as scientists worked to understand how ESP operates."

While not proof-oriented, this screening has always been respectable. "Less than half of the 30,000 letters my mother received met those requirements and were accepted for inclusion in her database." That rough attrition rate still holds true to this day.

Further investigation is clearly preferable. The Society for Psychical Research in England published the first major collection of spontaneous ESP experiences in 1886. Entitled *Phantasms of the Living*, this monumental, two-volume work featured 702 reported ESP experiences. Each one was carefully investigated, verified, and authenticated in an effort to provide evidence for the existence of telepathy. With this proof-oriented approach, the investigators for the Society for Psychical Research also preferred ESP experiences that had been written down soon after they happened, or at least told to someone else, while memories were fresh. They also proactively sought out character references who could vouch for the experiencer's character and honesty.

Unfortunately, the Rhine Research Center hasn't the time, staff, or money to investigate every possible ESP experience sent in. The days of independently wealthy, upper-class gentlemen pursuing the study of possibly paranormal claims out of pure curiosity are over. One recent radio interview alone generated 60 new experiences people wanted to share with Dr. Feather. She screens and answers as many as she can. Millions more await her. A 2001 Gallup Poll found that 25 percent of all Americans – that translates into 65 million people – report having an ESP experience. If even one percent emailed her, she'd be flooded with half a million stories.

In Cynthia's case, however, the experience was dramatic enough to entice me into a little digging.

Her story seems consistent with known facts.

Serial killer Michael Ross was born, lived, worked, and killed six of his eight victims in a relatively confined area of eastern Connecticut – all within an hour of the town where Cynthia herself lived at the time of her encounter. Some snatchings were uncomfortably close. One 19 year-old girl was killed in the town of Norwich, a five-minute drive from Cynthia's house. Another four victims came from the town of Griswold, just 20 minutes down the road. Ross clearly trawled Cynthia's home turf for victims.

Ross primarily targeted teenage girls. Five of the six Connecticut victims were age 17 or younger (two were 14 years old). The 15-year-old Cynthia fits the profile of his preferred victim.

Ross grabbed all six Connecticut girls while they were

hitchhiking or walking along the road, just like Cynthia was doing that day. Victim Robin Williams was last seen thumbing a ride when she disappeared; Deborah Taylor had run out of gas and was backtracking down the road to find a filling station when she was abducted; Wendy Baribeault was walking down State Highway 12 to a convenience store; April Brunais and Leslie Shelley were walking home from the movies together; Robin Stavinsky disappeared while hitchhiking in Norwich. Cynthia had skipped school that day and was hitchhiking to the mall.

Ross wasn't committing murder in the winter of 1979, when Cynthia had her encounter with the "insurance salesman." He killed his first known victim – a co-ed at Cornell – in the spring of 1981, over a year later. But court documents do confirm that Ross was already stalking and raping women by 1979.

Still, some parts of her story puzzled me, so I phoned Cynthia.

The story sent to us didn't say anything about her ESP going off when he first picked her up. I found that somewhat odd. Cynthia explained that she *had* sensed something very wrong with the man that day but didn't know how to extricate herself from the situation. "I didn't want to freak him out by asking him to let me out of the car. I felt very vulnerable."

She filled in additional details of that day. The man said he would teach her how to drive a car, and they ended up in nearby, deserted Mohegan State Park – an ideal place for a rape if the stranger had that on his mind. But Cynthia's turn at the wheel was short-lived. The car skidded on the ice and she hit a guardrail. He seemed nervous about the car. She pointed out it was getting late and he said he would drive her home.

Why would she let him take her home? Wasn't she afraid he would find out where she lived? Cynthia had an explanation. "The school books I had on the front seat of the car had my name on them. All he had to do was look up my address in the phone book. So he already knew how to find me. Also, it was late, and I needed to get home quickly. He couldn't return me to school, because I knew the school bus had already left for the afternoon." She had him drop her off across the street from her house, but her brother saw her get out of the car. When her parents asked about her ride, she told them he was a man she had met at their local hospital, where Cynthia sometimes volunteered as a Candy Striper. He was a nice guy, she reassured her parents. An insurance agent.

That turned out to be a mistake, and the reason Cynthia gives for her subsequent, puzzling agreement to go out on a date with him. Her parents were very excited that their rebellious daughter had finally found someone decent to go out with, instead of the bad crowd she hung around with. They pushed her to accept a date. She felt trapped. "I felt a tremendous pressure not to disappoint my parents," she says.

How eager were they to make it work? When her well-dressed date showed up at the house, her parents rolled out the red carpet for him – in this case, a seat of honor on the prize gold sofa in the formal living room the family used only for special occasions. Under this significant pressure, Cynthia was actually resigned to going through with the date until the moment when, "like the snap of a finger," she simply "knew" without the shadow of a doubt, the man she was looking at meant to do her harm. From that moment on, nothing her parents could say, or threaten, or do could make her leave the house with him.

The next day, according to Cynthia's uncle Bob, her mom was on the phone to her sister bemoaning the "poor judgment" Cynthia exhibited by turning down such a "nice guy."

Coincidentally, shortly after my interview with Cynthia, I mentioned her experience to a friend of mine in Hawaii. It turned out that his brother, Patrick Clifford, was the Superior Court judge in New London, Connecticut who actually sentenced Michael Ross to death – and Judge Clifford had a strange experience of his own. At 2:01 AM, Friday, the 13th of May 2005, the judge woke with a start from a deep sleep – at the precise moment they gave Ross the lethal injection at Osborn Correctional Institution in Somers, Connecticut.

●●●

Psychic intuitions or impressions like the one Cynthia got are accompanied by a strong feeling of certainty, of conviction that the warning must be immediately acted upon. More intense conviction is associated with these sudden hunches, in fact, than with any other form of ESP. They're also quite common, making up about a third of the 14,000 reported spontaneous ESP experiences in the Rhine database.

In a neat bit of synchronicity, the day after Dr. Feather and I shared Cynthia's scary story on *Coast to Coast AM*, a 58-year old woman who had been listening in Seattle sent us an email. Janet (not her real name) had her own story to share – one she says that has "haunted me for over 30 years."

It turned out to be another woman's possible brush with a serial killer. She wrote:

> I was twenty four at that time, and living in Seattle, Washington in a suburban house on Sand Point Way, a busy road that leads from the U. of Washington to the north end of Seattle. It was Valentine's Day, 1969.
>
> I had been turning the soil over in my garden that morning. It began to rain so I went in the house for lunch. My dining table was by the window that looked out at ground level on the front walk. I looked up and saw a really good looking, well-barbered, well-dressed young man standing at the window staring at me. I was married to a pretty disreputable hippie then, and the two of us lived a very uninhibited life style. The man staring in my window was a really good looking guy and in those days that was sometimes all the introduction necessary.
>
> In those days my boundary awareness was woefully lacking. I never locked my doors; friends were encouraged to just walk on in. I would open the door to strangers and chat with them. I was not the timid type. I even used to hitchhike down to San Francisco by myself.
>
> So nothing should have made me afraid of him. Yet something immediately compelled me to race to that door as fast as I could and put the chain on it. It was

completely out of character for me. But I felt absolutely he was a danger to me.

I opened the door a crack and asked the man what he wanted. He said he knew my husband, and that my husband had told him it would be OK to stop in and use our phone if he was in the area. The man said this in the most polite, sincere and charming way.

I remember thinking I was being totally irrational, but the feeling of panic was simply overwhelming. I said 'No!' and slammed the door on him and locked it.

He stood looking through the window as if he were weighing the situation. I went to the phone and picked it up; he could see me do it. As I began to dial, he ran – he didn't walk, he raced – to the street and I saw him jump into a light colored VW bug and drive off.

Later, my husband said he had never met the man I described, let alone say he could use our phone. Shortly after that I left my husband and moved to Bainbridge Island.

Five years later, when pictures of serial killer Ted Bundy started appearing in the media, I recognized the man who had come to my door.

I sometimes lie awake at night and wonder why I was warned. There have been other instances of ESP in my life, but this one taught me to listen to that voice of warning. I am sure it saved my life.

She added a P.S. " Thanks for letting me tell you this, I have been carrying it around for years and haven't told it to many people – it almost is too unbelievable."

Fascinated by the similarity of Janet's experience to Cynthia's, I googled serial killer Ted Bundy's life. Called the "poster boy for serial killers," Bundy admitted to murdering 40 women in a dozen states over a period of four years in the 1970s.

Matching up Janet's creepy experience with what I learned about Bundy's murderous method of operation, I discovered her description of the man she met and the events she described fit Bundy quite well.

At the time of the encounter, Janet matched Bundy's typical victim profile: young, Caucasian, light brown hair parted in the middle.

Bundy was a student at the University of Washington, and Sand Point Way is a major highway leading from the university to North Seattle. So it's likely he passed up and down the street Janet lived on.

Janet described the man at her door as "a really good-looking man" who spoke in a "polite, sincere, charming way." Almost everyone who encountered Bundy described him in the exact, same way. Stephen Michaud, author of *The Only Living Witness: The True Story of Serial Sex Killer Ted Bundy*, found women who met Bundy routinely described him as "sincere" and "courtly around women…. More than one woman used the term 'beautiful' to describe Ted Bundy." At his trial, groupies swooned and some women even sent him letters asking to marry him.

Janet didn't notice him until she saw him "standing at the window staring at me." Bundy admitted to the police that he often stalked the streets of the Seattle/Tacoma area – where Janet lived – "peeping into women's windows."

When he stalked women, Bundy "approached them on a pretext," a method of operation eerily similar to Janet's stranger who tried to gain entry into her house by asking to "use the phone" since he was in the area.

Finally, when the panicked Janet picked up the phone, the stranger "ran to the street, and I saw him jump into a light-colored VW bug and drive off." According to Bundy biographer Michaud, "(Bundy's) happiest moment during his first year of college came when he bought a '58 Volkswagen bug for $400. The little car meant freedom to Ted. He could get in it and drive and be alone whenever he wanted, a reprise of his early boyhood when he and his collie, Lassie, would disappear out into the trees for hours. Ted loved VWs. He would own two in his life; the second one, a light brown '68, eventually would yield evidence of his secret life." The stranger Janet locked the door on not only drove a VW bug; it was a "light-colored" car.

Janet was "90 percent sure it was him." She had been saved from Ted Bundy.

The evidence suggests it might have been him. But Janet is wise to leave a margin for doubt.

At one point, I was convinced it couldn't have been Bundy. According to one biography I found on the internet, at the time Janet encountered the stranger knocking on her door, Feb. 14, 1969, serial killer Ted Bundy was supposedly living in Philadelphia, Pennsylvania, attending Temple University. It's hard to be in two places at once. Case closed?

Ironically, Dr. Feather's good friend is well-known paranormal writer Leslie Rule, author of *Coast to Coast Ghosts* and *Ghosts Among Us: True Stories of Spirit Encounters*. Her mother, bestselling crime writer Ann Rule, wrote the definitive biography of Ted Bundy, *The Stranger Beside Me*. Hoping to confirm Bundy's whereabouts that Spring, I telephoned Leslie and asked if she could check with her mom. It turns out that Bundy did visit Philadelphia during that period, but there's no record of him spending all Spring there. Case re-opened a crack.

But Leslie added a word of caution. "When my mother's book came out, she got hundreds of stories from women who believed they had escaped death at the hands of Ted Bundy." A serial killer on the prowl can appear to be everywhere.

For her part, Janet knows who she saw that day. "The guy left an indelible picture in my memory from the incident." She majored in graphic design in college. "I am a very visual person. I remember people's faces, even when I meet them only once."

If Janet were wrong about the stranger being Bundy, might her intuition have still been right – that the polite, young man at the door, Bundy or not, intended to do her harm?

Janet reports a history of puzzling intuitions that have come true. "I have had many instances of 'knowing' – the account of the man at my window was of course the most dramatic," she explained to Dr. Feather in a follow-up email. "One very early instance I remember was as a child. My pet cat didn't come home one evening and my family was worried about her. I got a very clear picture in my mind of the cat lying on the side of the road above our house. I insisted that my dad go look there. He took a flashlight and found her exactly as I had said. Unfortunately she was dead – hit by a car. I had known that too, but I had so hoped it wasn't true.

"A happier incident was in 1990. I saw in one of our local stores a drawing for a trip to France. I have never really felt inclined to enter any contests but I 'knew' I would win this one. I told my husband as I was writing my information on the slip that we would be going to France. He thought I was silly. The day of the drawing came and went; I didn't hear anything and I was really very puzzled because I had seldom 'known' anything so acutely. Two days later the phone rang – it was the store congratulating me for winning the big prize. My husband doesn't doubt my 'knowings' anymore."

So the stranger at her door that Valentine's Day in 1969 could have meant her harm; she's had intuitions come true. But it's also possible that the young man really wanted nothing more than to make a phone call.

In the end, we're left hanging. Did Janet and Cynthia save themselves from death at the hands of two of America's most notorious serial killers, or simply chase off two poor souls frightened by false intuitions? Short of an expensive, time-consuming, professional investigation, we'll never know for certain.

One can understand why most parapsychologists, frustrated by such ultimately inconclusive human experiences, have turned for solace to the repeatable lab experiment. But leaving a large portion of reported reality unacknowledged and unexamined is fundamentally dishonest science, not to mention unfair to people like Janet and Cynthia who show the courage to share their experiences. One way or another, we must find a way to deal with these stories. To paraphrase Fox Muldar, "The experiences are out there," they're in the millions, and they show no signs of going away.

MICHAEL SCHMICKER is co-author with Dr. Sally Rhine Feather of *The Gift: ESP–The Extraordinary Experiences of Ordinary People* (St. Martin's Press, 2006, paperback). His first book was *Best Evidence: An Investigative Reporter's Three-Year Quest to Uncover the Best Scientific Evidence for ESP,*

Psychokinesis, Mental Healing, Ghosts and Poltergeists, Dowsing, Mediums, Near Death Experiences, Reincarnation and Other Impossible Phenomena That Refuse to Disappear (iUniverse, 2nd Edition, 2003). Readers can learn more about both books by visiting booksbymichael.com

ELUSIVE TELEKINESIS:
THE RUDI SCHNEIDER STORY
By Gregory Gutierez

In 1924, Dr. Eugene Osty became the second director of the Institut Métapsychique International, the French equivalent of the Society for Psychical Research founded in England. In 1929 and 1930, Osty conducted some 90 controlled sittings with the well-known Austrian medium Rudi Schneider. For the first time in the history of psychical research, Osty's experiments were not simply seeking to convince others of the reality of psychic phenomena on the basis of the testimony of famous and honorable scientists or writers, but rather he attempted to design a device that would not only produce scientific data but also protect against, and possibly uncover, potentially fraudulent behavior.

By the end of the 1920s, Osty had made considerable progress since his first experiments in so-called "objective" psychic research (the French term "metapsychique objective" was coined by the famous French scientist Charles Richet in his volume *Traité de Métapsychique* as a label for the study of physical phenomena occurring during spirit trances). In 1926, Osty had invited the Polish medium Jean Guzik to the Institut Métapsychique International to carry on a new series of séances. Osty thought it was necessary to continue the work on Guzik that had been carried out by his predecessor Gustave Geley, as the controversy about the "Manifeste des 34" and the séances at the Sorbonne in 1923 had left many outstanding questions and frustrated many of the scientists. Furthermore, in 1925, bad news had come from Poland; during séances held by the Psychic Society in Krakow, a picture had been taken without Guzik's knowledge. The picture showed his left hand free of any bonds, hovering over the table. So, if Guzik ever was a genuine medium, he nevertheless could lose his power and had to cheat in order to satisfy the scientists.

Was Guzik just a fraud who succeeded in deceiving several

important French observers and thus implicated in a great sham? Eugène Osty wanted to get to the bottom of it. Between March and May 1926 he therefore organized new séances with the Polish medium. Osty succeeded in convincing a physicist, who wished to remain anonymous, to photograph the séances in the ultraviolet, so as to seize the phenomena on the spot, in darkness, without upsetting the medium during the séance.

Unfortunately, Guzik's stay in France ended between the demonstration séances and the first – inconclusive – tests of Osty's device. Political disturbances forced Guzik, a family man, back to Poland. Out of the forty or so séances that had been carried out, Osty considered about twenty of them to be "good," especially the first ten. Unfortunately, they happened to be the "let us see what happens" séances, during which Guzik was only controlled by his hands and legs, and always by two persons, which might have enabled him, just as in Krakow, to free up one of his hands. (How? See page 30.)

Osty nevertheless claimed to be convinced by the "ideoplastic" phenomena of Jean Guzik, even if he was careful not to declare them scientific truths: "Guzik left Paris on May the 20th, our projects having not been carried out. Nothing can thus be changed in the public opinion. People will keep on believing or not believing the reality of Guzik's phenomena from the same information. What I was able to witness has confirmed in me the opinion that Guzik, put in a position where he cannot cheat and in adapted conditions, is likely to produce paranormal action over matter, but I have no scientific proofs whatsoever enabling me to try and communicate my beliefs to other people."

The relative failure of those experiments from a scientific perspective did not discourage the new director of the Institut Métapsychique. For some time, Osty had been hearing about the alleged exceptional séances held by two young Austrian brothers, Willy and Rudi Schneider. In 1923, Baron Von Schrenck-Notzing, the respected Munich psychiatrist, observed Willy Schneider's gifts in his laboratory and gave them a positive review. In 1929, during a lecture at the Institut Métapsychique, British psychical researcher Harry Price reported the results of several séances organized with the youngest and most discreet of the boys, shy Rudi. It was very probably right after this lecture that Osty decided to invite Rudi to the Institut Métapsychique to work with him. But before reviewing the details of those experiments, one must understand the works and personality of Harry Price, whose role would prove essential in what was to soon become "the Schneider Case."

Rudi Schneider and "Uncle Harry"

Born in London in 1881, Harry Price was fascinated by occultism, conjuring, and ghost stories. He gradually gathered an impressive collection of works on those subjects; at his death in 1948, the collection he left to the London University consisted of no less than 18,000 volumes. In 1908, Price married a rich heiress and was able to completely dedicate himself to his passion, visiting alleged haunted places and meeting spiritualist mediums. He became famous after his skeptical enquiry into the well-known spiritualist photographer William Hope, whose pictures showed faces of dead people around the portraits of persons he photographed. Price succeeded in showing that Hope used previously exposed photographic plates in order to produce these out-of-the-grave apparitions.

In 1920, Price became a member of the Society for Psychical Research (SPR), then in 1923 he founded an independent scientific entity, the National Laboratory for Psychical Research (NLPR). There he organized séances with a young nurse, Stella Cranshaw, an English version of the physical medium Eusapia Palladino. The table was lifted up on several occasions, sometimes violently, but more than that, from the reports of the fearless researcher, the medium managed to switch on an electric connector placed under a glass bell, pompously named the télékinétoscope. Price appealed to the press without hesitation, often inviting journalists to take part in his enquiries or in the séances held in his laboratory. This kind of constant self-promotion did not suit the leaders of the SPR who considered the NLPR a kind of rival society and Harry Price a researcher who, despite his obvious knowledge, preferred newspapers headlines to scientific publication.

In 1929, Price published a long article in the journal of the NLPR, in which he expressed his wish to see all psychic societies close ranks and, needless to say, have him as their leader. To this end, he got in touch with nearly all the active European researchers, including Eugène Osty in Paris who politely turned down his proposition, as did all the other researchers.

That same year, Price had young Rudi Schneider come to London for a series of séances. In order to avoid any fraud, he had designed a device of electrical control, simple in its principles but complicated in its functioning, from an idea he borrowed from a certain Karl Krall, a fellow worker and friend of Schrenck-Notzing. During the séance, the people taking part had to put on metallic gloves and slippers that were so tight they were very hard to take off afterwards. The slippers had to rest on metallic bars fixed to the ground, and each person held the hands of their two immediate neighbors, thus enabling a feeble electric current to run in the circle formed by the participants. As soon as one of them let go of a hand or moved a foot away, the circuit would break and a light would signal their position on a control panel.

Of course, young Rudi was himself submitted to this control, as was Harry Price who was alone in charge of the physical control. Facing Rudi, Price seized his hands and stuck Rudi's knees between his own legs. This manner of physical control by a single person prevented the already famous fraud which consisted of having a *single* hand controlled by *two* persons, one holding the wrist and the other the fingers of the *same* hand without knowing it. In those controlled conditions, but almost in darkness, Price got several impressive phenomena inside and around the spiritualist cabinet, while Rudi was a certain distance away, near the spectators. As with Eusapia at the beginning of the century, the curtains waved violently, some spectators felt sudden gusts of wind and chilly draughts. On several occasions, a "pseudopode," a kind of half-shaped hand, emerged from the curtains to seize objects lying on the ground. A lean whitish figure the size of a man was observed moving behind the curtains, even as Rudi Schneider was still firmly held by Harry Price.

Price's electrical control system, as ingenious as it was, nevertheless had two major defects. On the one hand, it was impossible for the people present to make any gesture whatsoever without breaking the circuit, making them powerless spectators of the scene. On the other hand, an electric lead would sometimes break or someone would inadvertently move a foot, causing an interruption of at least fifteen minutes, the time necessary to fix the circuit with the light back on, which in turn would cause Rudi to come out of his trance. This system, even if it prevented Rudi from moving his hands or feet, made the séances particularly laborious. Besides, the whole experiment was founded on the supervision and the control of Harry Price alone.

In 1930, after 27 séances, Harry Price published *Rudi Schneider: A Scientific Examination of his Mediumship.* The book's publication received nice media coverage, as Price had invited journalists to attend the experiments and had challenged the British illusionists: a thousand pounds to anybody who could reproduce the phenomena certified by the NLPR, under similar circumstances. Nobody took up the challenge, and more than that, in 1929, the illusionist Will Goldston, founder and head of the Magician Club, declared to the *Sunday Graphic,* after having attended one of the séances: "I am convinced that what I saw was not a fraud. None of my magician fellow workers could have achieved such effects, considering the compulsory conditions."

It was a media triumph for Harry Price, though Rudi Schneider certainly did not understand its full extent. Aged barely twenty when he first came to England in 1920, he could not speak a word of English and seemed particularly shy. He nicknamed the English researcher "Uncle Harry" and trusted him entirely. Besides, he left London just after the publication of the book to join Eugène Osty in France.

The infra-red device built by Osty

Rudi arrived in Paris on October 10, 1930, bathed in London glory, but probably apprehensive at arriving, once again, in a country where he could not speak the language. Osty had developed a radically new method of control for the Austrian medium. With the help of his son Marcel, an engineer, Osty had designed a device that used infrared beams, which were reflected and directed by little mirrors coupled with cameras. The rays surrounded a little table on which were laid various small objects that Rudi would have to move via his alleged telekinesis power. If the medium tried to seize an object with his hand, the infrared beams, invisible to the naked eye even in obscurity, would be suddenly cut, causing the camera to photograph the event. Since neither the medium nor the spectators had to be controlled during the séance, this method spared the participants the tedious electric control used by Harry Price. This device also narrowed the focus of attention to a very precise experimental zone, limited by the rays, with the assumption from the beginning that no peripheral phenomenon would be taken into account.

Some months earlier, Osty had managed to test the efficiency of his system at the expense of a Polish medium, Stanislawa Popielska. In darkness, as the medium was announcing that the conjured ghost was about to produce a phenomenon, Osty triggered his camera. The picture showed Stanislawa, freed from her bonds, stretching her arm over the table to seize the object she was supposed to levitate! The picture of the medium caught in the act was later published in the November-December 1930 issue of the *Revue Métapsychique*. It was published with the account, by Osty, of the reactions caused by the discovery of the fraud. A good friend of the medium's, who had come with her to Paris, had begged Osty not to publish the picture for it would "cause prejudice to psychic research" and because the medium's husband, a convinced skeptic, might murder his wife if he learned of the fraud! The husband, left in Poland, far from harboring ideas of murder, gave his own explanation of the picture, summed up by Osty in these words: "If a hand was seen out of the bonds, it is because the bonds happened to have dematerialized, a phenomenon he [the husband] was convinced that eminent Polish psychics could attest the reality of, and that he would ask the Court to take these psychics as arbitrators."

First séances with Rudi Schneider

The séances with Rudi Schneider at the Institut Métapsychique started on October 11, 1930, the day after his arrival in France. Before entering the room, Rudi was undressed and dressed with pajamas bearing fluorescent stripes on the sleeves and trousers. He then sat facing Eugène Osty, who controlled Rudi's hands and feet, just as had done Harry Price earlier. Next to them were some people sitting in a row of chairs. On a high table, about one meter away from Rudi and behind him, was a white handkerchief, a flower, and a bell. During the first séances, which were designed to "see" how the medium "worked", the table was not yet controlled by the infrared beams, as the goal was mainly to observe Rudi's behavior. A weak, adjustable, orange-colored ceiling light lit up the table and its surroundings. Osty told Rudi to intercede with "Olga," the spirit who would inhabit his body during the trance and who would move the objects. To follow her movements in the darkness, the curtains of the spiritualist cabinet were adorned with fluorescent stripes on their borders and a little bell at the bottom. Because of translation problems, Osty did not think it was necessary to explain to Rudi the exact nature of the controls. The young Austrian only knew that he was, once again, the subject of concern to scientists wishing to witness strange phenomena.

The spirit of "Olga" then entered Rudi. At times, she said she was Lola Montes, an adventurer who had her hour of glory in America, performing episodes of her own life on stage. But when asked precise questions about Lola Montes, she was never able to give the right answers, as Schrenck-Notzing had noticed before. According to Osty, other than a real spirit, perhaps it was a second personality emerging thanks to the séances, issued from what he called Rudi's "cryptic conscience."

The difference of mood and personality was obvious between Rudi, a very shy young man, and his double Olga, quite an inconsiderate lady resembling Eusapia's "John King." Olga used to ask the people present to create a joyous atmosphere, to have fun, to hum songs or to talk of this and that. She sometimes stopped the séance to demand that people change places. She even sometimes asked people she disliked to leave. Olga usually required a break every fifteen or twenty minutes for Rudi to rest before turning to more serious issues. Then, an entire hour could pass before anything happened, waiting with awkward singing and Olga's regular promises for the appearance of phenomena.

During the trance, changes occurred to Rudi's physical and mental state. He would become very intense, his breathing quick and automatic, until the end of the séance. His breathing was often compared to the noise of a train engine. During the séance, Rudi remained prostrate, leaning against his controller. He was sometimes shaken by sudden nervous reflexes and streaming with sweat. At the beginning of the 1920s, during the search of the medium's body at the end of the séances, Schrenck-Notzing reported finding seminal liquid inside the young boy's pants. But Osty did not comment on that strange situation.

The first séances with Rudi at the Institut Métapsychique led to mixed results, far from the brilliance the medium had displayed to date, even if some discreet phenomena happened anyway. During the third séance, the people present observed what looked like a "dense grayish fog" coming from the curtains on the floor, then reaching the table before disappearing quickly. During the fifth séance, the table moved about twenty centimeters under the eyes of those present, who also heard it creaking. During the tenth séance, the curtains softly undulated, making their little bells ring. At the twelfth séance, the curtains moved again, then swelled until they reached the table, pushing it and eventually knocking it over. Finally, during the thirteenth séance, the curtains moved lightly again. Nevertheless, Rudi remained perfectly visible in the red light, sitting on his chair, in his fluorescent outfit. For Osty, this was quite a disappointment. The objects on the tables were never moved, despite Olga's constant assertions that "the Force" was about to seize them. The timid movement of the curtains was nothing compared to the violent gusts attested to by Schrenck-Notzing or Harry Price.

What was wrong with Rudi? The archives of the Institut Métapsychique show a correspondence between Osty and the Austrian Gerda Walther, who was Shrenck-Notzing's secretary until his death in 1929. Gerda knew Rudi and his family very well. On November 28, 1930, Osty wrote: "It is true that Rudi Schneider, in a bad period of mediumship, has given the Institut only two positive séances (a telekinesis, a vision of a mass, the aspect of fog, the moving of a table). But they were enough, considering the seriousness of the control, to give me the complete assurance that Rudi S. is really gifted with the powers of a medium. I claim this with my mind perfectly at ease. Photographic records of the phenomena, by the way of invisible rays, have not been made yet, for we wish the medium to get acquainted to the place and things, and because the phenomena have been too rare."

Occurrences of the "invisible force"

Osty decided to send Rudi back home in Braunau, Austria, for the Christmas and New Year celebrations. Before he left, probably upset by Osty's disappointment, the young medium insisted on having a new séance on the 10th of November. None of the classical phenomena happened, but for the first time Osty used his infrared beams and camera control system. A new high table, screwed to the floor, was set up with only the white handkerchief on it. The séance started at 10:35 pm. At 10:45, Olga announced that she was about to create a phenomenon that could be photographed. At 10:48, she said that "the force" was "going from the cabinet to the table." A moment later, the first flash of magnesium lit up the room. Olga explained that the sudden light prevented her from lifting the handkerchief and asked for Rudi to break for a rest. The séance started again at 11:30. At 11:52, Olga told those present that the séance would have to go on, regardless of how tired Rudi was. A second flash of magnesium. Some minutes later, Rudi came out from his trance and the séance was delayed.

When Eugène Osty developed the two photographs, he saw only ordinary scenes. The people present were on their seats, Rudi was visible, prostrate, his back facing the table, the mirrors reflecting the beams were in their right place… and the handkerchief was still on the table.

So what then triggered the cameras at the precise moments when Olga was stating that "the Force" was about to act? Osty suggested a possibility: "As soon as the people were gone, we checked our devices to look for the reason the magnesium might have spontaneously degraded. We found nothing. The whole system, very well put to the test before the séance, seemed to be perfectly working after the séance. We thought that Rudi, in his often useless efforts to lift objects by a psycho-physical work, might exteriorize a substantial kind of energy – what he calls "the Force" – too subtle to be photographed, and whose presence in the infrared beams absorbs enough of their radiance to trigger the automatism leading to the deflagration of the magnesium."

The following day, a new séance took place, but this time, in order to avoid being interrupted by sudden flashes of magnesium, the beams were associated with a bell, very much like the ones used on telephones at the time. The ringing was set to go off when the beams were "absorbed" -- that is to say when their intensity diminished by at least 30 percent of their initial value. Osty kept the control on the cameras thanks to a switch.

The séance started at 3:45 p.m. Nine minutes later the phenomenon occurred. When Olga announced that the Force was coming close to the handkerchief, the bell rang. At the second ringing, Osty took a picture. The séance started again at 4:19. The bell rang again many times, for up to 44 seconds in a row, and always whenever Olga announced that the Force was coming to or from the table. After a while, Olga suggested that the table be unscrewed, promising that she would be able to lift it. The séance started again at 5:30. Olga agreed to warn the audience when to take the picture.

5:41 : Olga-Rudi -- The Force is coming out.

Ringing for 5 seconds, then brief pauses during 27, 3, 12, 18 seconds.

Olga-Rudi -- I will try to lift the table.

The ringing goes on for 100 seconds, while Doctor Osty awaits the agreed sign to deflagrate the magnesium.

5:46 : Olga-Rudi -- Hold tight with the chain of hands, the Force is about to become quite big.

Ringing for 52 seconds.

New announcement of coming out of Force, new prolonged ringing.

While the bell is ringing, and as the subject groans and shakes, he is asked whether it is time to take a picture, in case he has forgotten. He answers yes, quite weakly.

A flash of magnesium. The ringing is at once less strong, but only stops 2 seconds after the flash.

Olga-Rudi -- The Force cannot resist the light, it suddenly goes in the cabinet then out of it.

This time the table did not levitate. Neither would it do so during the 77 séances that took place after January 1931. Nevertheless, Eugène Osty thought he had witnessed the famous "psychic Force" observed by Crookes about sixty years before, which had since been renamed "telekinesis" by Charles Richet. Even if not visible in photographs, the Force could absorb infrared beams it went through when coming out of the spiritualist cabinet curtains. According to Osty, the discovery was all the more convincing since young Rudi ignored the nature of the controls he was submitted to.

On November 4, 1930, Rudi finally came back from Austria. On January 12, 1931, Gerda Walther wrote to Osty: "Between Christmas and the New Year, Rudi gave some very lovely séances in Braunau, which I witnessed. I am sending you a report of two of them, written for the Austrian paper *Das Neue Licht*. After my departure, there was a Farewell séance for Major Kalifius who happened to be in Braunau for a few days. I was told that this séance was impressive. So I hope that the new séances in Paris, starting now, will be much stronger that the ones last year."

During 1931 Doctor Osty carried on his séances with Rudi Schneider. He performed 77 of them, for a total of no less than 93, including the first ones that were not recorded and during which the "psychic energy" was revealed. It is probably the longest series of experiments a medium has ever been submitted to.

Wishing to insure that the Force was indeed confined to a specific place, Osty then modified his system, creating two independent sources for the beams instead of one. One beam passed in front of the table, the other behind it. Under those conditions, Osty was able to determine that, when Olga announced "the Force is coming out from the curtains and to the table," for example, it was indeed the beam closer to the curtains that was absorbed, and not the one passing in front of the table.

Then Osty sought to determine the beam's maximum rate of absorption when the Force crossed it. He obtained a maximum value of 70 to 75 percent of its initial intensity. The infrared beam was then never completely cut, as it would have been if a solid and opaque substance had crossed it. Rather it seemed to be stopped by a vaporous obstacle, a kind of gas or invisible smoke, which condensed or expanded following Olga's directions. Cigarette smoke could produce a similar absorption profile.

During the séances, Osty's efforts mainly focused on Rudi's physiological state. He first noticed that the occurrences of the psychic Force were always accompanied with strong muscular tensing. Then he took some interest in Rudi's hyperpnea, this abnormal increase in the depth and rate of breathing, which recalls a steam engine or the frantic panting of an animal. While in normal state, Rudi took about twenty breaths a minute. While in trance, he could reach 350 breaths, and was able to keep this rhythm for almost one hour. Hyperpnea produces a sudden flow of oxygen to the brain and causes dizzy spells and fainting fits. But for Rudi, the hyperventilation lasted for a very long time, and he finally got used to it after a few minutes.

In order to study the link between this atypical breathing and the emission of the Force, Osty placed a stretchable cloth belt on Rudi's chest, linked to a cylinder-shaped Marey drum, so as to obtain a precise measure of his respiratory amplitude. During the séances, the absorption of the beams was recorded graphically. Osty found out that the strength of the Force was in sync with Rudi's breathing. It was strongest just after Rudi inhaled and decreased as Rudi exhaled. This suggested there may be a narrow link between over-oxygenation, a constant muscular tension, and the coming of the Force. These observations led Osty to consider three hypotheses:

"Considered as a whole, the human body is a tank and a transformer of surrounding energy. When a being like Rudi Schneider produces a form of energy of an exceptional biological kind, one has to think that he is doing nothing more than operating an exceptional transformation of his inner energy. From which part of his body does it come? This will have to be answered in order to reach the truth as soon as possible, starting from hypotheses suggested by facts, and judging of their value by means of experimentation.

"The recordings made during the séances raised three main hypotheses."

First hypothesis: "The energy coming out of Rudi comes from his central nervous system; which is subjected to a functional overexcitement by the hyperpnea…"

Second hypothesis: "The muscle structure in Rudi's body is the biological factory supplying the energy (and not the nervous system)…"

Third hypothesis: This combines the two previous hypotheses. "Rudi's cryptic consciousness uses the hyperpnea to overexcite the central nervous system that produces the release of usable energies in the muscle structure. This new energy is then unleashed outside the body in order to produce the phenomena."

Thanks to his observations of Rudi Schneider, Eugène Osty is probably one of the first psychic researchers to have tried to explain telekinesis in biological terms, to find a rational explanation for it. Universal law says that nothing is created, nothing is lost, everything is transformed, so is it possible that the "psychic force" comes from an enigmatic nervous or muscular kind of fast-breeder reactor that would produce enough energy for apparently incredible phenomena? In the beginning of the 1930s, this avenue of research initiated by Osty seemed promising. Unfortunately, the never-ending controversies about psychic research would soon return and seal the end of an era.

At the beginning of the summer of 1931, Rudi Schneider went back to Austria once again. He planned to return to Paris in October, as Osty wished to continue the séances in order to better understand the link between the medium's respiratory rhythm and the absorption of the infrared beams. During his stay in Braunau, Rudi held several séances with Gerda Walther and Harry Price. At this time, Osty had already published the results of his experiments in the *Revue Métapsychique* and Harry Price had already heard about them.

On August 31, 1931, Gerda Walther wrote to Osty to inform him that "two very nice séances" had taken place in Braunau with Price in attendance. The English researcher apparently offered Rudi to go to England: "Rudi does not seem very eager to accept Mr. Price's invitation to go to London in September; it is then highly improbable that he will go. I hope you have made some lovely improvements with your report of the experiments with Rudi and that you will have nice phenomena when he comes to Paris next October."

Rudi indeed went back to Paris for some new séances until December. At the beginning of 1932, Osty and his son presented their work in a book entitled *Les pouvoirs inconnus de l'esprit sur la matière: Premières étapes d'une recherche. (The Unknown Powers of Mind over Matter: First Steps of a Research Project).* But at the same time, the Institut Métapsychique was facing important financial problems. Supporting Rudi Schneider for a whole year had cost the Institut Métapsychique a lot of money and the donors and sponsors were beginning to be hard to find. In the *Revue Métapsychique*'s last issue of 1930, an article entitled "Help us" called on the readers' generosity to put up the money for new equipment. But in January 1932, Eugène Osty had to tell Rudi – who had been in Austria for the New Year – that the Institut Métapsychique would have to stop the study of his mediumship because of money problems. The following month, Rudi met up with his "Uncle Harry" in London.

Rudi Schneider Exposed!

Before Rudi's arrival, Harry Price had received a confidential letter from his fellow researcher at the Institut Metapsychique. In May and June 1931, Miss Mitzi Mantl (or Mangl), Rudi's young fiancée, took part in some séances during which no noticeable phenomenon was recorded. Nevertheless, Osty and his colleagues had quickly become suspicious of the young woman's ambiguous behavior. On January 15, 1932, Eugène Osty warned Harry Price: "If I remember correctly, you had the idea of making his girlfriend come to London also. It is because of this recollection that I am writing this letter, asking you to keep it confidential.

"I would like to advise you not to let the young lady attend the séances. When there are no phenomena, she will try to provoke them. You could meet some disappointment and unpleasant incidents. She was in Paris in May and June. We did not want her to come in October.

"I almost told Rudi about the danger there was for him to make such a compromising person attend the séances. In the end, I thought I might upset him and so I did not. Was I wrong? But I wanted to warn you so that you would be able to take precautionary measures.

"Rudi is an honest boy whose talent is very safe and who accepts every kind of control. The girl has tried to make us take some of her cheatings for real phenomena, which was quite useless because we were only relying on what was happening within a space where cheating was impossible."

From February to May 1932, Harry Price organized 27 new séances with Rudi Schneider at his National Laboratory for Psychical Research. Yet despite Osty's warning, he chose to invite Rudi's fiancée to attend those new séances. This time, Schneider's coming was well covered by the British papers. The séances utilized a reproduction of the infrared beam system invented by Osty. The system was then perfected by Professor C. L. Gregory, the head of the department of astronomy at London University. Out of the new séances, eight turned out to be completely fruitless, but during the nineteen others, the attested phenomena were similar to the ones reported by Osty. As before, the infrared rays were interrupted at the precise moment Olga-Rudi announced the actual action of the Force.

Cameras placed at several places in the laboratory took pictures very much like the ones Osty had taken in his laboratory the previous year. Some of them even showed the handkerchief on the high table at the moment when it was clearly sliding across it, as if pulled or pushed by an invisible force.

By this time, the Society for Psychic Research, having taken interest in the young Austrian since the publication of Osty's results, got in touch with him to hold new séances, independently of those organized by Price. This invitation did not please Price, who had known for some years about the severity with which the SPR members judged the whiff of scandal of his public stands. In 1931 Price had tried once again in vain to convince the members of the SPR to merge their society with his national laboratory. He also now had some reason to bear Eugène Osty a grudge, too. Not only had the head of the Institut Métapsychique politely declined his offer to merge their two societies in 1929, but also, since Osty's discovery of a psychic force emanating from Rudi's body, Price's previous works with the medium had been overshadowed.

In May 1932, a controversy broke out between several researchers of the SPR and Harry Price himself in the columns of *The Times* about the recent séances at the NLPR. At the same time, Price sent several letters to Rudi's father in Austria to make him persuade his son to turn down the SPR's invitation to work with them. And in a "personal and strictly confidential" letter addressed to Rudi himself, Price went as far as explicitly threatening him: "You would regret it all your life."

In spite of those insistent warnings, Rudi agreed to work with the SPR. New séances were organized between October and December 1932 under the auspices of Lord Charles Hope. They confirmed again, even if less obviously, the strange phenomenon of absorption of the infrared beams. But the publication of these works in the *Proceedings* of the SPR followed a sensational article, written in such haste some weeks before by Harry Price in his own review of March 5, 1933, that he even chose not to warn the other members of his society about this article.

In this text, Price disclosed an incriminating photograph, taken during a séance on April 28, 1932. Rudi's left arm, freed from its controller, was stretched behind his back, as if the medium was trying to seize the handkerchief on the table! But the picture was quite fuzzy and the circumstances in which it was taken seemed very strange. According to Price, it looked like a double exposure, two pictures printed on the same glass plate, because of a functional problem with the camera at the time. The figures are indeed doubled, including Rudi's, clearly visible in his pajamas, leaning toward his controller, Price himself.

Another strange detail: Rudi's hand could not be seen emerging from his sleeve. In its stead there is a black patch where the border of the sleeve seemed to have merged. Yet, nothing hides the border of the sleeve and no shadow seemed to explain this black patch. Furthermore, Price explained that on this day the second camera broke down and he could not get a second photograph of the same scene, as he did for every other photograph at the time. Finally, this "proof" wasn't published until one year after the séance, at the moment when, by chance, the results of the series of experiments at the SPR were disclosed. Yet, in the interim, Price several times defended the quality of his séances with Rudi Schneider, without ever mentioning any doubt on the reliability of the controls.

Anita Gregory, the SPR historian who wrote a book on the Rudi Schneider case, expressed serious doubts about the authenticity of the picture, raised questions as to the circumstances of the shot, and about the exact role Price wanted the photograph to play. Checking the records of the researcher in the library of the University of London, she has discovered the original print of the famous photograph, which is far sharper than the copies shown in the papers in 1933. She raised a very curious detail about Rudi's feet: their position did not match the rest of his body. According to Gregory, Price had deliberately tried to make a forgery from several existing pictures so as to discredit his protégé and to damage the reputation of the SPR.

Could Harry Price sacrifice Rudi Schneider for such a petty goal, in a complete fabrication? The notion is not as absurd as it seems, considering that Price was suspected of forgery in at least one other case. In 1929, the psychic researcher had made an enquiry about a haunted monastery in ruins, the allegedly haunted Borley Rectory. When he came back on the scene with a journalist fifteen years later, in 1944, he wrote a book about the enigma of this famous haunting. During their visit, the journalist photographed a mysterious "flying brick." It would later come to light that Price, hidden behind a half shattered wall, had thrown the brick himself!

So apparently Harry Price did not hesitate to distort the facts for his own interests. His disconcerting way of accusing Rudi Schneider could account for the fact that he might have forged the incriminating picture himself. Nevertheless, the secret reasons for this accusation were far from being as obvious in 1933 as they would be later on. At the time, the discovery of a photograph "proving" an attempt at cheating by the most famous medium embroiled European psychic researchers in a series of controversies in the media, which they would rather have avoided. In April 1933, Eugène Osty published in his *Revue Métapsychique* a long article entitled "The Strange Behavior of Mr. Harry Price," in which the head of the Institut Métapsychique, usually so diplomatic, no longer hid his feelings toward Price: "As long as Mr. Price was unmasking false mediums and established hoaxes, I thought it a duty to back him in the *Revue Métapsychique*, as I am one of those people who think that mythomaniacs have to be put out of our way, and that psychic research has nothing to fear of those repercussions. But today, I cannot bear to see a genuine medium, submitted to the most rigorous controls, being the victim of a mania of exhibition and of a childish hatred toward the Society for Psychical Research."

Osty added to his article a note written by Professor Jules Bois, who was at the time head of the National Laboratory for Psychical Research, which was founded by Price. Bois made clear that no member of the NLPR was consulted before the publication of the upsetting photograph, whose existence was completely unknown to them at the time. Price acted alone, without consulting the directing committee. Besides, several members of the organization who attended the séance of April 28, 1932, took a stand against Price in the English newspapers. They claimed to have no recollection of the event captured by the questionable photograph and could not explain Price's sudden change of mind, as he had until then always defended the authenticity of the phenomena and the quality of the controls on Rudi Schneider during the NLPR séances.

The young Austrian was put to the test by the SPR one last time between October 1933 and March 1934. During this period, the 54 séances were entirely negative. Not once were the beams interrupted, in spite of Rudi-Olga's allegations on the action of the psychic "Force." As often happens in the study of mediums, when there are no results, the failure was explained away by the gradual disappearance of the medium's psychic talent, which is a very convenient but not convincing explanation. Yet, that same year, during séances held in Austria, the SPR investigators admired some impressive displays of the phenomena of telekinesis with the same Rudi.

The controversy around Rudi Schneider, Harry Price's complex personality, Eugène Osty's perseverance (nearly a hundred séances were organized in one year), his questionable but nevertheless upsetting study of the "Psychic Force" -- all these elements were emblematic of the situation of psychic research at the beginning of the 1930s. Rudi Schneider was the last of the "great mediums" on whom researchers had placed so many hopes. After him, European research into mediumship seemed just to mark time, as if exhausted by controversy and deceived hopes.

REFERENCES

Anita Gregory (1985), *The Strange Case of Rudi Schneider*, Scarecrow Press.

Harry Price (1930), *Rudi Schneider: A Scientific Examination of his Mediumship*, Methuen & Co.

Eugène Osty (1931), *Revue Métapsychique,* n°6, pp 393-427.

Eugène Osty (1932), *Revue Métapsychique*, n°1, pp 01-59.

Eugène Osty (1932), *Revue Métapsychique*, n°2, pp 81-122.

Extracts of personal letters by Gerta Walther and Eugène Osty, Archives of the Institut Metapsychique International of Paris.

GREGORY GUTIEREZ, a French journalist and Fortean, is a member of the French Institut Metapsychique International. He lives in Paris and founded the French discussion group Liste Aleph, dealing with fortean news and debates since 2002. He also manages a group of independent researchers from different specialties to conduct UFO research projects. He published the book *Les Aventuriers de l'Esprit – Une histoire de la parapsychologie* (Presses du Chatlet, 2005) written with the collaboration of Nicolas Maillard. Gutierez wishes to thank his friend Aline Cannet for the help she provided in the English translation of this text.Gregory Guitierez's blog, dealing with fortean topics, can be found at http://www.greguti.com/myblog.

OPERATION ESPIONAGE:
A COLD WAR TALE OF
PSYCHICS, SPIES, AND UFOS
BY NICK REDFERN

Many people who have examined the history of the U.S. government's relationship to the fields of Extra Sensory Perception and Remote Viewing have assumed that research began in the early 1970s with the groundbreaking work of Harold Puthoff and Russell Targ. Countless books and thousands of pages of officially declassified documents point towards that conclusion. Those same books and documents demonstrate that the CIA, the Defense Intelligence Agency, and the U.S. Army all began to dig deep into the mysteries of the mind in that particular era, primarily in an attempt to determine how effective ESP might be as a tool of espionage. In reality, however, as will now become apparent, official U.S. interest in psychic spying began *decades* before the 1970s.

It scarcely seems feasible to imagine that, on a summer's afternoon in August 1957, a seemingly innocuous suite in the Marriott Hotel on US Highway 1, Arlington, Virginia, was the location for potentially historic, and almost-out-of-this-world, activity that attracted the high-level interest of the U.S. intelligence community. That this same high-level interest focused upon three alleged teenage psychics and an employee of the local railway company seems even more bizarre. Just occasionally, however, truth really is stranger than fiction.

The weird saga encompasses government agents, official secrets, and revolutionary powers of the mind, and had its origins in the early 1950s with the controversial UFO contactees George Adamski and George Van Tassel. Born on March 12, 1910, in Jefferson County, Ohio, George Wellington Van Tassel maintained that he experienced face-to-face contact with some very human-looking alien entities following a claimed encounter in August 1953 near his Yucca Valley home in California. The complete history of Van Tassel's exploits with alleged extraterrestrials is quite bizarre, involving weird accounts of meetings with imaginatively named aliens, including Numa of Uni, Ah-Ming of Tarr, Rondolla of the Fourth Density, and Zolton, the Highest Authority in the Sector System of Vela.

As a result of his alleged August 1953 encounter, Van Tassel compiled the first issue of what he titled *The Proceedings of the College of Universal Wisdom*, a small journal that served as a mouthpiece for Van Tassel and his supposed cosmic friends. In the first issue, Desca, like Rondolla, also of the Fourth Density, urged Van Tassel's followers (whose number would very quickly reach four figures) to "remove the binding chains of limit on your minds, throw out the barriers of fear [and] dissipate the selfishness of individual desire to attain physical and material things."

In the edition of the *Proceedings* dated December 1, 1953, Van Tassel stated that, less than a month previously, a "message was received from the beings who operate the spacecraft," with orders from Ashtar, "the Commandant of Space Station Schare" (pronounced Share-ee), to contact the office of Air Force Intelligence at Wright-Patterson Air Force Base, Dayton, Ohio. Van Tassel went on to advise the Air Force that: "The present destructive plans formulated for offensive and defensive war are known to us in their entirety...the present trend toward destructive war will not be interfered with by us, unless the condition warrants our interference in order to secure this solar system. This is a friendly warning."

Were Van Tassel's contacts genuinely of unearthly origin? Were they the rants of a sadly deluded mind? Or were they possibly a part of a sophisticated Communist-inspired intelligence operation designed to disrupt the internal security of the United States? This third possibility was definitely of concern to a Yucca Valley resident who on August 5, 1954, wrote to the FBI suggesting that Van Tassel be investigated to determine if he was working as a Soviet spy. Seriously concerned that Van Tassel was either a witting or an unwitting player in an ingenious, but subversive, Communist plot, the FBI sought to ascertain the full picture. On November 12, 1954, Major S. Avner of the Air Force's Office of Special Investigations met with N. W. Philcox, who was the FBI's point of liaison with the Air Force, to discuss the growing controversy surrounding Van Tassel. Three days

later, Avner re-established contact with Philcox and advised him
that the Air Technical Intelligence Center at Wright-Patterson Air
Force Base "has information on Van Tassel indicating that he has
corresponded with them regarding flying saucers."

Very probably this was a reference to the letter that Van Tassel
wrote to ATIC at the request of the mysterious Ashtar, who had offered
a "friendly warning" with respect to plans formulated for offensive
and defensive war. As a result, and not surprisingly, the Air Force

offered "to furnish the Bureau with more detailed information."

One day after Major Avner of AFOSI spoke with Philcox, two Special Agents of the Los Angeles FBI office met with Van Tassel at his Giant Rock home. In a memorandum to FBI Director J. Edgar Hoover dated November 16, 1954, the agents wrote: "Relative to spacemen and space craft, Van Tassel declared that a year ago last August, while sleeping out of doors with his wife in the Giant Rock area, and at about 2.00 a.m. he was awakened by a man from space. This individual spoke English and was dressed in a gray one-piece suit similar to a sweat suit in that it did not have any buttons, pockets, and noticeable seams. This person, according to Van Tassel, invited him to inspect a spacecraft or flying saucer, which had landed on Giant Rock airstrip. Van Tassel claimed the craft was bell shaped resembling a saucer. He further described the ship as approximately 35 feet in diameter and is now known as the scout type craft. Aboard this craft was located three other male individuals wearing the same type of dress and identical in every respect with earth people.

"Van Tassel claims that the three individuals aboard the craft were mutes in that they could not talk. He claimed they conversed through thought transfers, and also operated the flight of the craft through thought control. He stated that the spokesman for the group claimed he could talk because he was trained by his family to speak. The spokesman stated that earthmen are using too much metal in their everyday work and are fouling up radio frequencies and thought transfers because of this over use of metal. According to Van Tassel, these individuals came from Venus and are by no means hostile nor do they intend to harm this country or inhabitants in any manner. He declared they did not carry weapons, and the spacecraft was not armed. He mentioned that a field of force was located around the spacecraft which would prohibit anything known to earth men to penetrate. Van Tassel claims this craft departed from the earth after 20 minutes and has not been taken back since."

Van Tassel added that, "through thought transfers with space men," he had been able to ascertain that a third world war was on the horizon, which was likely to be "large" and "destructive;" that much of this correlated directly with certain biblical passages; that the war would not be "universal;" and that the "space people are peace loving and under no circumstances would enter or provoke a war."

●●●

George Adamski, who was born in Poland in 1891, told a similar story. Adamski had the distinction of being the most supported, celebrated, and ridiculed of those who claimed direct contact with human-like extraterrestrials in the 1950s. The controversy largely began on November 20, 1952, when, along with six other people, Adamski claimed that he witnessed the landing of a UFO in the Californian desert and then made contact with its pilot. FBI documentation, however, showed that Adamski's interest in UFOs preceded the 1952 date by at least two years.

At the beginning of its surveillance of George Adamski, the FBI did not apparently have any awareness of his earlier claims of contact. However a document dated May 28, 1952, references his supposed 1950 encounters, and also reveals that – as with Van Tassel – the FBI considered Adamski to be a subversive. A study of the documentation shows that much of the FBI's initial data on Adamski came from a source (whose name the FBI has chosen to keep classified) that revealed the facts to its San Diego office on September 5, 1950:

"[Source] advised the San Diego Office that he first met Adamski about three months ago at the café which is named the Palomar Gardens Café, owned and operated by Adamski, at the road junction, five miles East of Rincon, California, at a point where the highway branches off leading to Mount Palomar Observatory.

"[Source] became involved in a lengthy conversation with Adamski during which Adamski told them at great length of his findings of flying saucers and so forth. He told them of a spaceship which he said he saw between the earth and the moon, which he estimated to be approximately three miles in length, which was flying so fast that he had to take about eighty photographs before he could get three of them to turn out.

"According to [source] Adamski stated that the Federal Communications Commission, under the direction of the 'Military Government' of the United States, has established communication with the people from other worlds, and has learned that they are so much more advanced than the inhabitants of this earth that they have deciphered the languages used here. Adamski stated that in this interplanetary communication, the Federal Communications Commission asked the inhabitants of the other planet concerning the type of government they had there and the reply indicated that it was very different from the democracy of the United States. Adamski stated that his answer was kept secret by the United States Government, but he added, 'If you ask me they probably have a Communist form of government and our American government wouldn't release that kind of thing, naturally. That is a thing of the future – more advanced.'"

Adamski's comments that his alien friends were communists at the very least caused raised eyebrows within the FBI and led to continual monitoring of his activities. Indeed, the FBI's surveillance of Adamski was taken to a whole new level when the crime-fighting agency recorded that: "Adamski made the prediction that Russia will dominate the world and we will then have an era of peace for 1,000 years. He stated that Russia already has the atom bomb and the hydrogen bomb and that the great earthquake, which was reported behind the Iron Curtain recently, was actually a hydrogen bomb explosion being tried out by the Russians. Adamski states this 'earthquake' broke seismograph machines and he added that no normal earthquake can do that.

"Adamski stated that within the next twelve months, San Diego will be bombed. Adamski stated that it does not make any difference if the United States has more atom bombs than Russia inasmuch as Russia needs only ten atom bombs to cripple the United States by placing these simultaneously on such spots as Chicago and other vital centers of this country. The United States today is in the same state of deterioration as was the Roman Empire prior to its collapse and it will fall just as the Roman empire did. The Government in this country is a corrupt form of government and capitalists are enslaving the poor."

From that moment on, Adamski was officially considered by the FBI to be a "security matter." In a meeting with both the FBI and the Air Force of Special Investigations that occurred on January 12, 1953, Adamski said that on November 20, 1952 out in the deserts of California, he had a close encounter of a very unusual kind, as the FBI carefully noted in a report prepared for FBI HQ:

"At a point ten and two-tenths miles from Desert Center on the road to Parker and Needles, Arizona, Adamski made contact with a space craft and had talked to a space man. Adamski stated that he, [deleted] and his wife Mary had been out in the desert and that he and the persons with him had seen the craft come down to the earth. Adamski stated that a small stairway in the bottom of the craft, which appeared to be a round disc, opened and a space man came down the steps. Adamski stated he believed there were other space men in the ship because the ship appeared translucent and could see the shadows of the space men."

Adamski also revealed that the alien was "over five feet in height, having long hair like a woman's and garbed in a suit similar to the space suits or web suits worn by the US Air Force men." And just as George Van Tassel had done, Adamski related to the FBI and OSI agents that he conversed with the being by means of sign language, but felt that his mid was being "read."

It is important to keep in mind that both Adamski and Van Tassel had made the claim that their alien visitors communicated with them by telepathy or by some form of ESP. And it is equally important to note that both men were investigated by the FBI to determine if they had communist leanings, or were even – wittingly or unwittingly – spreading propaganda on behalf of the Soviet Union.

According to Richard Duke, a 1950s specialist in psychological warfare, the FBI had begun to receive, as far back as 1949, "reports and stories" very similar to those of Adamski and Van Tassel – to the effect that human-like aliens were among us and, worse still, that they were communists. However, says Duke, the FBI came to a startling conclusion: that the claimed encounters with Red extraterrestrials had nothing to do with visitors from other worlds. Rather, the FBI believed, they were the result of the Soviets having perfected a form of mind-control and "brain-to-brain contact" in which U.S. citizens were being "implanted with thoughts" by Russian "mind-soldiers" to the effect that they were having real-life experiences with aliens who wanted to tell us how wonderful communism was.

In reality, Duke elaborates, the experiences were "stage-managed, psychological warfare" and were simply the effects of highly sophisticated "mind-management and manipulation" by the Russians of unwitting citizens, who may very well have believed precisely what they were saying. Moreover, Duke claims that the Russians had apparently acquired "the skills to do this" from Nazi scientists captured at the end of World War II who had been working to perfect the utilization of such "mind phenomena" for Adolf Hitler, who was indeed known for his interest in the paranormal.

Duke maintains that this theory came to ultimate fruition in 1952, specifically after cleared FBI agents had attended "two of seven or eight" lectures that had been held in the Pentagon that year on just such a use of ESP for psychological warfare purposes. That such lectures in the Pentagon *did* occur, and that the U.S. intelligence community *was* aware of Hitler's interest in such matters, is not in doubt. In 1977, in a document titled *Parapsychology in Intelligence*, Dr. Kenneth A. Kress, an engineer with the CIA's Office of Technical Services, wrote: "Anecdotal reports of extrasensory perception (ESP) capabilities have reached U.S. national security agencies at least since World War II, when Hitler was said to rely on astrologers and seers. Suggestions for military applications of ESP continued to be received after World War II. For example, in 1952 the Department of Defense was lectured on the possible usefulness of extrasensory perception in psychological warfare."

Another source that confirmed the 1952 ESP lectures at the Pentagon was Andrija Puharich, an American of Yugoslavian descent who began to investigate ESP in 1947 at a laboratory he had founded in Glen Cove, Maine. In 1959, Puharich stated that during August 1952 he was contacted at his Glen Cove lab a by representative of the U.S. Army who wished to speak with him about his research into ESP: "A friend of mine, an army colonel, who was Chief of the Research Section of the Office of the Chief of Psychological Warfare, had dropped in to say hello. He expressed a rather normal sort of curiosity about my investigations of extrasensory perception and was quite interested in a device which we had been developing in order to increase the power of extrasensory perception. The colonel then surprised me by saying that if we found any positive results to be sure to let him know, as the Army was definitely not disinterested in this kind of work."

Puharich continued: "It was November 1952 before the statistical analysis of the telepathy experiment was completed. The results showed that extrasensory perception was increased in the Faraday Cage device by a healthy margin over those scores obtained under ordinary room conditions. My enthusiasm led me to send the results to my colonel friend in the Army. He invited me to give a report on this work at the Pentagon. On November 24, 1952, I made such a report before a meeting of the Research Branch of the Office of the Chief of Psychological Warfare. As far as I could tell at the time my report evoked little interest in this group."

According to Richard Duke, however, the presumed lack of interest in Puharich on the part of the military was merely a ruse. In reality, the Army and the CIA, in particular, had a deep interest in the subject and in trying to determine if ESP offered significant applications for the military and intelligence communities. However, Duke adds, "the military and the Company jealously guarded its discoveries" from the FBI, due to the fact that "there were rumors around the Pentagon that someone in the FBI who was looking into this because of the Contactee things had been turned by the Russians and was reporting back to them on what [the Pentagon] was learning about what they, the Russians, were doing in this ESP game."

Therefore, says Duke, beyond confirming to the FBI that, yes, ESP *might* be a potentially valuable tool from a psychological warfare perspective, there was a big reluctance on the military's part to share too much data with the FBI that could potentially be of value to the perceived Russian mole that some Pentagon officials feared was buried deep within the FBI. The result was that, with the Army only willing to share snippets of data, the FBI began its own studies of the phenomena. Those studies, Duke elaborates, followed a path that was similar to the military and the CIA's – trying to determine how effective ESP might be for espionage purposes. And a study of available documentation that has surfaced via the Freedom of Information Act does seem to confirm that the FBI "was never really given the full picture by the Army."

● ● ●

Midway through 1957 startling data came to the attention of the FBI, which, if true, had the potential to radically change the world of espionage overnight and forever. It was on July 16 of that year when a document titled "Extra Sensory Perception" was prepared by the assistant director of the Bureau's Domestic Intelligence Division, Alan H. Belmont, who was then the acknowledged "number three man" within the crime-fighting organization. Circulated to, among others, the Assistant Director of the FBI, Cartha DeLoach, the document outlined the story of a man who exhibited apparently extraordinary skills: "One of our agents attended a private exhibition of extra sensory perception given by Mr. William Foos at American Legion Headquarters in Washington, D.C. This exhibition was informal and attended by twenty individuals, principally officials of the Veterans Administration.

"Mr. Foos, resident of Richmond, Va., is a high school graduate employed in a minor capacity with the C. and O. Railway. About two years ago he became interested in extra sensory perception (a term probably technically inaccurate) and began experimenting with members of his family. He claims to have achieved amazing success and in recent weeks has received a considerable amount of publicity in the Richmond area. He is holding a number of exhibitions locally in an apparent attempt to create interest in his ability to teach the blind to see. He has appeared at Duke University where experiments have long been conducted on the power of extra sensory perception, and various government agencies (including the Veterans Administration) are very much interested.

"Very simply Foos claims the ability to teach the blind to see; in six months to teach a person without eyes to see sufficiently well to drive an automobile safely. He disclaims any supernatural power and, not being a scientist or physician, has no technical or scientific explanation. He merely states that a person can do what he makes up his mind to do. He claims to have taught not only members of his family but approximately 25 other individuals as well, including persons completely blind, to see with 100% efficiency."

The document continued: "To illustrate his ability, his daughter, Margaret Foos (about 16 – 17 years of age) was blindfolded by the observers with pads and an elastic band, thereafter reading, distinguishing color and moving about the room with complete ease. She could read minute handwriting submitted by those in attendance, accurately trace the written material and in all ways function without error as with complete vision. In answer to a question as to whether distance was a factor, Foos stated that during one recent public exhibition Margaret had distinguished colored balloons at a distance of 400 feet. In answer to another question as to whether motion would complicate the problem, Margaret played the childhood game of jacks using a small (1½" diameter) rubber ball, deftly retrieving it regardless of angle of bounce.

"Mr. Foos was questioned as to his ability to teach a person to read an article covered by a pad or to see through a wall. He at that time avoided a direct answer, stating that because of the defense aspects of such a possibility he was not at liberty to discuss it. Later, however, he claimed that he had taught one of his students to accurately read an article completely obscured by heavy cardboard and that teaching the ability to see beyond a solid masonry wall was merely a matter of degree. He would pursue this matter no further.

"[The FBI agent] inquired of Foos as to his general method of teaching – whether individual tutoring was essential. He stated that he had taught a group with equal facility. He further stated that he had found it much easier and had had greater success in teaching the physically blind rather than those with ordinary vision."

In a partly blacked-out section of the document, Belmont both recognized and enthused upon the seemingly endless applications that Foos' talents offered the murky world of international and domestic espionage. Indeed, one can almost imagine Belmont positively salivating when he stated: "Should his claims be well founded, there is no limit to the value which could accrue to the FBI – complete and undetectable access to mail, the diplomatic pouch; visual access to buildings – the possibilities are unlimited insofar as law enforcement and counterintelligence are concerned. As fantastic as this may appear, the actuality of extra sensory perception has long been recognized – though not to the degree of perfection claimed by Mr. Foos. It is difficult to see how the Bureau can afford to not inquire into this matter more fully. According to [Deleted], Bureau interest can be completely discreet and controlled and no embarrassment would result. It is recommended that the FBI make further inquiry of [Deleted] claimed ability to teach the blind to see, bearing in mind the tremendous potential to the FBI should these claims prove well founded."

Evidently this was of considerable interest to the FBI, and no doubt as a result of its experiences with the military at the Pentagon several years earlier. A heavily blacked-out document of August 13, 1957, demonstrates that the FBI dug very deeply into the Foos story. The Bureau even dispatched agents to pay secret visits to various libraries in the area in which Foos lived, as it sought to determine if any data was on file concerning publicity afforded Foos in his hometown. The Special-Agent-in-Charge at Richmond, Virginia informed J. Edgar Hoover: "The records in the library of the *Richmond Times Dispatch* and the *Richmond News-Leader*, newspapers of Richmond, Virginia, were checked on August 9, 1957, by Special Agent [Deleted], which reflected an article by K. Lewis Warren, date lined June 17 (1957), which related that Margaret Foos, a 16 year old high school girl, had demonstrated with her father, William Foos, of Ellerson, Virginia, methods by which William Foos hoped to teach the blind to read."

The FBI agent then went on to detail the nature of the demonstration. Cotton pads had been placed over the eyes of Margaret Foos, secured by a black elastic blindfold. And, in that condition, she had both located and read a passage from a magazine furnished by a reporter, and had also read samples of handwriting, as well as verses from the *Bible* that had been "request [sic] from the audience."

FBI HQ was also advised: "William Foos did not claim to be a psychologist or to have had even elementary knowledge of the subject; however, he claimed to have read everything possible on the subject of Extra Sensory Perception since starting his experiments some two years previous."

The FBI further learned that: "Foos had recently been to Duke University, where he had demonstrated for two days before Dr. Joseph B. Rhine, an eminent authority on the subject and other members of the Parapsychology Department of the University. The article then states that Foos impressed the viewers as being thoroughly sincere and stated that his main interest in his project is to help the blind; however, he refused to divulge his methods of teaching, but believed he can teach other instructors in the field. The article further sets out that FOOS hoped to obtain a charter for Extra Sensory Perception Research, Inc., and listed the backers and members of the organization as Henry Caravati, Richmond Public Relations Man, William Cantor, an auctioneer, and Robert Cantor, a lawyer. Further, if the charter was granted, Foos planned to recruit blind youngsters who would be willing to cooperate in the experiment."

As the FBI continued to dig into the story, it learned from other newspaper articles that just such a charter had indeed been granted: "The library contained another newspaper article, date lined June 22 (1957), to the effect that ESP (Extra Sensory Perception) Research, Inc., received a charter yesterday from the State Corporation Commission and will undertake clinical training for the blind."

The Bureau's research uncovered the full staff details of the organization, which was comprised of William Foos, President and Director of Research; Henry L. Caravati, Vice-President; Robert A. Lloyd, Vice-President; Sam Lombardo, Vice-President; Robert Cantor, Secretary; William Cantor, Treasurer; and Margaret Foos, Research Assistant.

The document concluded: "The staff was to leave Monday to conduct a series of demonstrations in Washington and New York and that a clinic would be opened when the staff returned." What was left unsaid in this document, but that would be elaborated upon later, was the intriguing fact that at least one of those "demonstrations" was undertaken explicitly for the benefit of the elite in the U.S. intelligence community.

In a report of September 6, 1957, titled "Extra Sensory Perception Demonstration by Mr. William Foos," Alan H. Belmont was advised: "According to information furnished to the Bureau, William Foos allegedly gave a demonstration in extra sensory perception to representatives of military intelligence and Central Intelligence Agency (CIA) sometime during August 1957. Pursuant to the request of Supervisor [Name Deleted], inquiry concerning this was made by [a] Special Agent [of the], Liaison Section, at the Office of the Assistant Chief of Staff, Intelligence (ACSI), Department of the Army.

"Lieutenant Colonel John Downie, Special Operations Branch, ACSI, advised [us] that a representative from the Army Intelligence Center at Fort Holabird, Maryland, had attended a demonstration given by Foos on August 8, 1957, at the Marriott Motor Hotel, U.S. Highway #1, Arlington, Virginia. Attached hereto is a copy of a memorandum submitted by George C. Blackwell, the representative from Colonel Downie's office attending this demonstration. As far as Colonel Downie knew, there was no representative from CIA at this demonstration; however, it was his understanding that on August 8, 1957, another demonstration was given by Foos to individuals unknown to Colonel Downie, not representing the Department of the Army, however."

According to Richard Duke, CIA operatives *were* present at the experiment at the Marriott Motor Hotel but the "Pentagon and the Company had their own reasons for not wanting to tell this to the FBI: ESP was their baby. The plan was to have the Army handle the domestic side in the States, and have the Company handle things overseas. But because the FBI kept digging, [the Army and CIA] knew they couldn't stonewall Hoover completely. So they gave his people parts of the story only, and made it seem like the Foos's were less credible than some in the military really thought they were."

And on the topic of the FBI's official sources in the military playing down the alleged successes of the Foos family, Belmont was also told: "Colonel Downie stated that Lieutenant Colonel Leroy C. Hill, the representative from the Army Intelligence Center, is making an evaluation of the demonstration; however, to date he has reached no conclusion. According to Colonel Downie, when Colonel Hill completes his evaluation, he, Downie, will so advise the Bureau. Colonel Downie further advised that his office has made inquiry from others who have attended different demonstrations put on by Foos with the following results: Inquiry was made with representatives from the President's Committee on Employment of the Physically Handicapped who attended one of Foos' demonstrations. It was determined that Major General Melvin J. Maas, U.S. Marine Corps (retired), Chairman of this Committee, was of the opinion that the claims by Foos that he could teach blind persons to perceive has not been proven by his demonstration and until such time as Foos has taught persons known to be blind to perceive objects, the President's Committee will not sponsor, recommend, or associate itself with Foos."

In conclusion, the report stated: "According to representatives of the Blind Veterans Association, who had attended one of Foos' demonstrations, the demonstrations did not reveal any extra sensory perceptive powers of Foos or any of his associates. That Association does not contemplate any action towards sponsoring Foos or his teachings."

Days later, another revelation surfaced that, in the eyes and minds of the Veterans Administration, cast considerable doubt upon the claimed powers of Foos and his allegedly psychic daughter, Margaret, as the ever-diligent FBI recorded: "Inquiry by Colonel Downie's office at the Veterans Administration reflects that the Veterans Administration, since Foos would not submit to scientific testings [sic] and since portions of the demonstration conducted with blindfolds furnished by the Veterans Association were 100 per cent unsuccessful, concluded that the claims of Foos were without basis. The Veterans Association contemplated no further action. Colonel Downie stated that the information from the Blind Veterans Association and from the Veterans Administration was obtained on a very confidential basis. He, therefore, requested that the Bureau not disseminate this information outside of the Bureau. Attached hereto also is a copy of a memorandum furnished by Colonel Downie relative to Dr. Henry K. Puharich, Round Table Foundation, Glen Cove, Maine. While Dr. Puahrich's work is not exactly in the field of extra sensory perception, Colonel Downie stated that the Army is interested in determining the possibilities of his techniques."

In part, the memorandum on Puharich states: "On 3 September 1957, Dr. M. K. Savely, Chief, Aero Medical Division, Air Force Office of Scientific Research, was interviewed in his office concerning [Puharich] and stated in substance: His only contact with [Puharich] was for about 2 days in August 1957 when he (Savely) and Mr. William J. Frye, Professor, Electrical Engineering, University of Illinois, visited [Puharich] in Glen Cove, Maine. [Puharich] directs from one to fourteen employees consisting of Peter Hurkos who was born in the Netherlands; Morey Bernstein who wrote *The Return of Bridie Murphy*; and others who act as domestic help. Dr. Savely was told by [Puharich] that the Round Table Foundation operates on contributions which average from $24 to $60,000 per year. Two of the Contributors and Backers are Representative Bolton of Ohio and Mr. W.K. Belk, department store owner from North Carolina. [Puharich] uses various electronic equipment and drugs in his experiments and appears to be dedicated to the study of the science of transmitting messages from one person to another through mental telepathy. [Puharich] graduated from Northwestern University in 1948 and served his internship at Permento Hospital somewhere in California. [Puharich] served in the Army Medical Corps in 1951-1953 at the Army Chemical Center, Edgewood, Maryland. Mr. Savely feels that [Puharich's] work is worthwhile and that [Puharich] could do some good in this field. Source knows nothing of a derogatory nature or anything concerning [Puharich's] political feelings or affiliations."

It is notable that, as was the case with Adamski and Van Tassel earlier, officials were interested in determining any links between Puharich's ESP connections and his "political feelings or affiliations."

● ● ●

But back to Foos. Were there good grounds for believing that "major doubt" had indeed been cast upon his claims of ESP? Or was this, as Richard Duke maintains, evidence that the military and the CIA were trying to make it appear that the activities of the Foos family were without merit, and that this would cause the FBI to lose interest in the subject? Whatever the truth, the FBI wanted answers – fast – and requested a copy of the official memorandum prepared by the Army as a result of the August 8 demonstration given by Foos at the Marriott Hotel, Arlington. Its contents made for intriguing reading within the FBI. Titled "Memorandum for the Record," it read:

"At 1400 hours, 8 August 1957, Special Agent [Deleted], accompanied Lt Colonel Hill to the Marriott Motor Hotel, U.S. Highway #1, Arlington, Virginia, to witness a demonstration of

Extra Sensory Perception. The demonstration was given in Suite 5008 (rooms 5005, 5006, 5007, and 5008) and was conducted by Mr. William Foos of Richmond, Virginia.

"Mr. Foos explained that, in February 1957, he inadvertently discovered a method of teaching others to see through barriers and distinguish objects beyond these barriers. He explained that his hope and intentions were to use this discovery in teaching the blind to see through Extra Sensory Perception, and that in teaching his daughter, Margaret, how to perceive objects etc., beyond physical barriers, he realized that this knowledge and ability had serious and dangerous implications as well as practical value in Military and/or Diplomatic operations. For this reason, he explained, he had limited the perceptory [sic] range of his pupils.

"Mr. Foos had Margaret seated at a card table and requested an observer to blindfold her. Two coats (cotton pads) were placed over her eyes and held in place with a dark elastic band that fastened behind the head. So blindfolded, Margaret demonstrated ability to read, distinguish colors, locate verses in the Bible, and trace handwriting. All objects read, traced or identified were placed on the table. Margaret was not successful in identifying or reading a Trip Ticket held approximately 16" above the table.

"A young man, approximate age 17 demonstrated his ability to identify ESP and playing cards before Special Agent [Deleted] and one other unidentified observer. The demonstration was held in the same manner – i.e. identical blindfold and cards placed on the table. This young man was approximately 50% successful in identifying ESP cards placed face up on the table, which he was allowed to feel and flex with his hands. His success in naming cards held up before him and facing away from him even without the blindfold was very limited.

"Special Agent [Deleted] is not qualified to judge on the ESP ability of any person in the demonstration. However [Deleted], feels that all demonstrations were merely tricks and can be explained logically by qualified performers in this field.

"Persons present in the demonstration were as follows: Mr. William Foos, alleged or self-styled discoverer of method of teaching ESP. Margaret Foos, daughter and pupil of Mr. Foos, age 16. Boy

– unidentified age 17. Girl – unidentified age 17. Demonstration was sponsored or arranged by Mr. Daniel Cox Fahey, Jr., 3805 Blackthorn, Chevy Chase, Md., Consultant, OSI, and Vice President, Washington Industrial Research Consultants."

Days later, specifically on September 6, 1957, documentation marked for the attention of future-Assistant Director of the FBI, Clyde Tolson, was generated that stressed the Bureau had "conducted a discreet background check on William Foos." Once again it emphasized the seemingly genuine psychic abilities of his daughter Margaret, and expressed concern about rumors to the effect that the unnamed teenage boy who was present at the Marriott Hotel demonstrations could "reportedly read documents which have been enclosed in a briefcase."

Admitting that the performances of the talented teens were "rather amazing," the FBI conceded that some of the personnel who had analyzed the data were of the opinion that everything was merely the result of "some trick." However, the Bureau was also careful to point out that even those skeptical of the demonstration were admittedly "unable to offer an explanation for the girl's ability to see while blindfolded."

Concerned, particularly, by the fact that someone might actually be able to read the contents (and, worse still, the *classified* contents) of a locked briefcase, Tolson demanded ultimate clarification on this issue. Interestingly, the unnamed agent that prepared the report played down the young boy's claimed skill and instead stated that: "…this was strictly a rumor which has been circulating around the Government and as far as he has been able to establish, there is no basis whatsoever indicating that a person can read beyond a wall." The CIA was evidently not so sure, however, as the FBI learned from its sources that the CIA "plans to follow any additional reports concerning Foos' work."

Matters took a downward turn for Foos, however, on September 17, 1957, when Belmont prepared a document titled "Extra Sensory Perception, Information Concerning," that focused specifically upon data that the FBI's "liaison agent" with the CIA had then recently uncovered about its observations and conclusions concerning Foos. One day previously, Bemont recorded, the liaison agent was informed by a representative of the CIA who had been assigned to "follow any reported developments of significance" concerning Foos, that in the Agency's opinion "Foos has not come up with any new or revolutionary development and his claims to certain performances in the field of extra sensory perception have not been supported by fact or evidence."

Things began to look even worse when the CIA informed the FBI that "Foos has insisted on using a particular type of blindfold which raises a question regarding the possibility that Foos is using nothing more than a trick by cleverly permitting his daughter to see by 'pinpoint vision.' [Deleted] is of the opinion that Foos is using a blindfold material which permits his daughter to have a considerable area of vision through a tiny aperture in the blindfold cloth.

"[Deleted] stated that it was interesting to note that Foos has refused to permit anybody to place any kind of a shield between his daughter's eyes and the document being read. He further stated that the daughter is able to read to certain extent while the blindfold is on her eyes but when the same material is placed face down on the document she is unable to read anything.

"According to [Deleted] he has conducted some research in this field and stated that with proper training a person can have a large field of vision looking through a small hole or even along the sides of a blindfold or disks which might be placed over the eyes. [Deleted] also remarked that although Foos claims to have an ability of training others in the field of extrasensory perception, he himself is unable to do any of the things which his protégés can do."

The FBI then began to look closer into the possibility that there was some sort of cunning deceit at work. A document from the files of Clyde Tolson of September 18, 1957, outlines the facts: "Numerous questions were asked of Mr. Foos following the demonstration and [our agent] was most blunt in his questioning in attempts to find out if there were any 'gimmicks' involved. Mr. Foos was quite evasive in his answers and refused to discuss his methods of instruction. He also refused to allow a demonstration of the young boy reading documents enclosed in a briefcase or reading through the walls of a room. He claimed, however, that this could be done and he would be willing to have this act performed at a later date."

Although the document stated that "Foos may, of course, be attempting to commercialize on a 'fake trick' he and his daughter and the young boy have perfected," it was also stressed that "On the other hand, there is a possibility that Foos does have extrasensory perception abilities. This, of course, is something we cannot afford to overlook in our work."

"But," the FBI added, "we should not, however, under any circumstances allow Foos the privilege of indicating to outsiders the FBI is interested in his work. He should be given no opportunity to use the FBI in any manner which would further his own interests." And so the debate rumbled on within intelligence circles for years without ever being full resolved to everyone's satisfaction.

There is no indication, however, that the attention paid to Foos in August and September 1957 by U.S. Intelligence was ever repeated, or that the FBI or the CIA ultimately employed the skills claimed by Foos and his daughter in any capacity. Indeed, the last entry in the part of the file that deals with the Foos affair, and that dates from 1960, states: "Recognizing the value of such activity to our counterespionage work, we thoroughly checked the claim and had to conclude that his alleged powers had no scientific basis."

But, as Richard Duke stresses, we may never really know if the FBI's decision to walk away from the Foos affair was due to the fact that the whole thing really *was* without merit, or if the FBI's actions and conclusions were prompted by the CIA and the Army's subtle attempts to convince Hoover and his Bureau that Foos, and the attendant controversy of ESP, were not worth looking into.

During this same time frame, the military was secretly expressing an interest in speaking with Andrija Puharich on this very issue. Consider the words of Puharich himself: "On September 12, 1957, a military friend of mine phoned from Washington with rather startling news. He said that he had been talking to some colleagues about our research in Maine and two officials had expressed an interest in visiting the laboratory. He told me that one of the men, a busy general, had picked a date to come to Maine. The date was September 27, 1957."

Ultimately, said Puharich, the planned visit was canceled. Richard Duke, however, maintains that the meeting *did* go ahead. Duke says that it was merely rescheduled and "went black" – a reference to the fact that Army officials did not want to have to admit to the fact that they were still digging into such controversies as ESP and psychic phenomena.

But the FBI was far from finished with the strange and twilight world of ESP. On June 14, 1960, none other than J. Edgar Hoover himself sent a memo to Tolson, Belmont, and DeLoach asking the question: "Is there anything to this?" The subject of Hoover's memo: an article by Ruth Montgomery titled "Spying By Mind-Reading" that had appeared in the *New York Journal American* that same day.

Forty-eight-hours later Belmont had prepared a reply for the attention of Hoover. The author of the article, it stated, "speculated that the ultimate achievement would be to develop a method whereby U.S. spies could 'receive' thoughts of plotters in the Kremlin. The Director asked, 'Is there anything to this?' Lieutenant Colonel Lee Martin, Chief of Investigations, Assistant Chief of Staff for Intelligence, advised liaison agent [Deleted] that the Army is conducting no such project as described in the article."

But did this mean that no such research had ever been initiated by the military? According to Martin, the answer was, unsurprisingly given the overwhelming secrecy that existed and still exists in the world of psychic espionage, not quite that simple. "He did state that the U.S. Air Force had a contract in 1958 and 1959 with the Bureau of Social Science Research, Washington, D.C., which did research in the many phases of mental problems raised by the Korean War, with particular emphasis on brainwashing. This research did incidentally include mental telepathy or extra sensory perception; however, the results were inconclusive."

Belmont continued that: "Our Laboratory experts advised that informed scientific opinion at the present time is that there is no basis in science for the validity of extra sensory perception as described in this article. It is true, of course, there are some areas and activities of the human mind which have not been explored or completely understood by psychologists for the purpose of explaining these little-understood functions of the mind."

Having reviewed the Bureau's files on the Foos affair, Belmont then added: "In 1957, one William Foos, Richmond, Virginia, claimed that he could teach blind persons to see through the use of extra sensory perception. He claimed he could teach people to read a paper which was covered or to see through a wall. Recognizing the value of such activity to our counterespionage work, we thoroughly checked the claim and had to conclude that his alleged powers had no scientific basis. Other Government agencies such as Veterans Association, Central Intelligence Agency and Assistant Chief of Staff for Intelligence also checked on Foos and were highly skeptical of his work."

Despite the fact that Lieutenant Colonel Martin had denied that the military was actively working on any ESP-based operations, Ruth Montgomery had apparently uncovered some intriguingly specific data about the Army program from an apparent insider source. Stressing that "top intelligence agents" were involved in the classified operation, Montgomery revealed: "The Army Intelligence Service is beginning to delve into an unknown reach of the mind which – should it eventually prove successful – could make spying the least hazardous branch of defense…The project receives expert guidance within the department, but many of the officers have become so fascinated by the possibility [of ESP] that they have formed groups, outside of office hours, to try reading each other's minds."

Montgomery continued: "Military intelligence for some time has been delving into the possible utilization of hypnosis in spying. This correspondent reported several years ago that intelligence agents were being sent on delicate missions; then brought back and queried in the normal manner about what they had observed. Afterwards, they were hypnotized, and while in trance were again questioned about the layout of the room they had been assigned to visit. Under this condition they were able to supply every detail, even down to the number of slats in the Venetian blinds. The drive to develop other techniques for espionage has been heightened, since the U-2 incident."

In conclusion, Montgomery wrote, "It would be pleasant to think that U.S. spies seated comfortably in Washington could pick up the dastardly plots that Communist big-wigs were hatching behind locked doors in the Kremlin. At least we can dream, can't we?"

Realizing that Montgomery had indeed made some very

definitive statements that suggested the military knew more than it was telling the Bureau (as Richard Duke has confirmed was the case), Hoover continued his probe into ESP matters. Two weeks later, on June 28, 1960, a document titled "Extrasensory Perception" was prepared for Assistant Director Tamm, which stated: "Director has commented about studies in extrasensory perception at Duke University. Experimental work in Parapsychology Laboratory there reported since 1934. Research has covered 'supernormal faculties' not recognized by modern psychological and physiological methods. Various forms of 'supernormal cognition,' telepathy, clairvoyance and precognition have been investigated using special ESP deck cards. Experiments devised for purposes eliminating pure chance as causative factor of evidence supporting ESP. Scientists generally critical of evidence and methods. Belief in ESP has gained little acceptance among psychologists and fails the test of common experience."

Tamm was further informed: "[Deleted] of the Parapsychology Laboratory, this university, has reported considerable experimental work in the field of psychical research. His experiments give the impression of psychological sophistication but have received continuous and severe criticism in learned circles since publication.

"Psychical research in parapsychology encompasses the experimental study of 'supernormal faculties,' real or supposed of human personality, supernormal being an equivalent for 'not recognized by general scientific opinion.' The function of this research is to collect and weigh all available evidence for and against such faculties, either for acceptance by general scientific opinion, or rejection. The theory supporting this investigation is completely opposed to results of research in experimental psychology which has not revealed other sensory mechanisms than those described in modern textbooks of psychology and physiology."

As the following demonstrates, FBI agents went to considerable lengths to acquaint Tamm with all of the relevant data known at that time on the subject of ESP: "The principle lines of investigation in parapsychology are directed for the most part in studying 'supernormal cognition,' that is knowledge shown by a 'percipient' (receiver) of matter concerning which he has no natural means of knowing. These include such debatable phenomena as: telepathy, supernormal knowledge derived from another's mind; clairvoyance, all manifestations of supernormal knowledge, not in the mind of another person, without the intermediary of sensory information; and, precognition, supernormal knowledge of future events that can neither be perceived sensorily [sic], inferred rationally or brought about deliberately. Because these modes of perception arise spontaneously from life experiences of certain persons only, the elimination of fraud, collusion and other sources of error are uncontrolled and uncontrollable. The devising of objective experimental techniques to establish reality of these mental phenomena presents difficulties not met in accepted psychological research."

According to the FBI, "laboratory experiments" at several unnamed locations had been made in three, specific areas, namely, clairvoyance, telepathy, and precognition. However, Tamm was careful to note that "In general, belief in extrasensory perception has gained little acceptance by informed scientists. Thus, replies to questions sent to members of the American Psychological Association recorded only two per cent responses expressing an opinion that ESP is an established fact, and seven per cent that it is a likely possibility. Ninety-one answered that ESP is a remote possibility, impossible or an unknown. However, the most valid objection against belief in ESP powers is that common experience does not produce evidence for telepathy, clairvoyance and precognition. For example, stock investments should prove most profitable ventures for anyone gifted with these so-called powers."

It wasn't until late 1960, explains Richard Duke, that Hoover – thanks to the carefully laid plans of the CIA and the Army – finally concluded that ESP was an issue that his crime-fighting organization should not be wasting its time on. Sure enough, documentation generated by the FBI in the final months of 1960 shows overwhelming skepticism on the Bureau's part in anything even remotely resembling ESP and psychic phenomena. As evidence of this, a document dated October 5, 1960, and titled "Statement by Director Concerning use of Extrasensory Perception in Solving Criminal Cases" began: "By letter to Director, 9-27-60, Edwin D. Krell, Midwest correspondent for Dell Publishing Company, advised he is planning to do an article concerning parapsychology in criminal investigation. He noted that much has appeared in newspapers on this topic in recent months, but in checking into the situation he found no evidence to support the contention that mediums have aided police in solving crimes. Kress feels the public is entitled to this information and requested a statement from the Director on this matter for use in the article."

The document continued: "Krell mentioned Gerard Croiset, a Dutch medium, who reportedly related what happened to Judge Joseph Crater, who vanished in New York in 1930. Krell also made reference to Peter Hurkos, also from Holland, who in June, 1960, made headlines while working on the Carroll Jackson family murder case. Krell noted that Hurkos' work led to the arrest of a suspect (John Atwell Tarmon) who was later released when the actual killer (Melvin David Rees, Jr.) was caught by the FBI.

"In conducting research into this matter, Krell advised he contacted a Dr. F. Brink, Dutch police official and attorney, who sent Krell an article he had written in which he stated: 'Neither in the Netherlands, nor in any other country, is it possible to obtain reliable information which would justify the conclusion that the judiciary authorities and the police derive any benefit from the intimations of clairvoyants.' Dr. Brink also quoted a letter from Scotland Yard: 'So far as the London Police are concerned, we completely ignore anything put forward by clairvoyants in the course of criminal investigation.'"

It is worth pointing out that, as I revealed in my 2003 book *Strange Secrets*, officially declassified files demonstrate that during World War II, the British Police Force used dowsers to locate the bodies of people killed in Nazi bombing missions on mainland Britain. The files make it very clear that the Police were very careful to ensure that this did not create, in the minds of the pubic, the idea that this was indicative of "support" for "the mysterious" in what was described as a "particularly dangerous" time.

To continue, internal FBI memoranda stated that the Bureau's files "reflect that Peter Hurkos, whose true name is Peter Cornelius Van Der Hurk, was born 5-21-11, in Dordrecht, Netherlands. He is alleged to have extrasensory perception and it has been claimed in many magazine and news articles that he has assisted police departments in many countries in solving crimes as a result of his ability. Bufiles [Bureau Files] contain no information to substantiate any of the claims made by Hurkos concerning the solution of crimes."

The document continues: "On 5-25-60, Dr. Francis Regis Riesenman, psychiatrist on the staff at St. Elizabeth's Hospital, Washington, D.C., advised the Virginia State Police (VSP) that he planned to bring Hurkos to Virginia and Maryland to observe the sites where the bodies of the Jackson family were found. He requested that the VSP allow Hurkos the opportunity of examining the clothing and other physical evidence in the case. VSP felt they would be subjected to public criticism whether they agreed or declined to participate and finally decided to allow Hurkos to examine the material. The Director noted: 'I am amazed that the VSP would participate in any such circus.'

This line from Hoover suggests that by 1960, as Richard Duke has noted, the military had convinced Hoover and his Bureau that ESP was an area that they should not trouble themselves with, as it was without merit. The FBI's skepticism of the early 1960s and onwards was further borne out by the following statement in the document: "Riesenman and Hurkos contacted the VSP on 6-7-60, and spent about a week working on the Jackson case, as a result of which the Director commented: 'We should be sure Hurkos isn't injected in which we have jurisdiction. He is a complete fraud.' The 6-9-60 issue of *The Washington Daily News* carried an article entitled Telepathist Says He Can See Killer which related that Hurkos stated he knew what the murderer looked like and hoped 'soon' to turn over to police information that would solve the case.' Mr. Tolson commented: 'This screwball is connected with the great Interpol.' The Director noted: 'How silly can one get?'"

According to Richard Duke, the FBI finally got the message. This, says Duke, allowed personnel from both bodies who were working in these areas to continue their clandestine studies "without Hoover's meddling." Duke states, however, that it *is* a fact that, a year or so later, research into what would later become known as remote viewing was indeed largely halted. He also states that it is also a fact that it did not recommence to any significant degree until the early

1970s with the work of Harold Puthoff and Russell Targ.

Rather disturbingly, however, Duke asserts that those "who had been working on the ESP project in the '50s," at the CIA and the Army turned their attentions away from relatively straightforward remote viewing to a much darker area of research; namely, trying to determine if the power of the mind could be utilized to kill – or, rather, assassinate – people. There were reportedly three areas of research being examined by this small CIA-Army group in the period 1961 to 1978:

(1) The use of ESP to induce chronic depression and anxiety in "foreign and domestic political figures" that would "hopefully" lead to suicide;

(2) Attempts to determine if psychic powers could be used to "guide" people to kill other individuals: "a kind of psychic Manchurian candidate," as Duke describes the situation;

(3) Research to determine the extent to which the human central nervous system could be affected by ESP, in an attempt to bring on fatal heart attacks and strokes.

Notably, Duke claims that in his opinion (and he stresses that it *is* only an opinion) the admittedly strange and large cluster of deaths in the 1980s and early 1990s of the British "Marconi Star Wars Scientists" and the post 9-11 deaths of numerous people all around the world who were connected to the field of microbiology may be the result of "trained and very effective psychic assassins doing their job for whoever wants these people gone."

The controversy surrounding the Government's involvement in ESP research may not be over. In fact, it could just be getting interesting – and, in the on-going climate of terror, very deadly, too.

REFERENCES

Strange Secrets: Real Government Files on the Unknown, Nick Redfern & Andy Roberts, Paraview Pocket Books, 2003.

The Sacred Mushroom: Key to the Door of Eternity, Andrija Puharich, Doubleday & Company, Inc., 1959.

On the Trail of the Saucer Spies: UFOs and Government Surveillance, Nick Redfern, Anomalist Books, 2006.

Extra Sensory Perception, 1957-1960 file declassified by the Federal Bureau of Investigation (FBI) under the terms of the Freedom of Information Act (FOIA).

NICK REDFERN is one of the world's foremost authorities on strange phenomena. His previous books include *A Covert Agenda*; *The FBI Files*; *Cosmic Crashes*; *Strange Secrets* (with Andy Roberts); *Three Men Seeking Monsters*; *Body Snatchers in the Desert*; and *On the Trail of the Saucer Spies*. He has written for *Military Illustrated*; *Eye Spy*; *Fate*; *Fortean Times*; *Phenomena Magazine*; and the London *Daily Express*.

LONDON'S MONSTER SCARES
By Hilary Evans and Robert E. Bartholomew

Every now and again, Londoners – like the citizens of any urban community – have suffered collective scares, causing them to respond by riot, panic or insurrection. Such incidents may be triggered by religious differences (e.g. the "Popish Plot" in the late 17th century in which genuine but vague concerns about Vatican conspiracy hardened into a supposed plot to kill the king) or by concerns of public health (Victorian Londoners were understandably suspicious of Thames water as a breeding-ground for cholera) or by many other threats to the community. Though the Scarlet Woman of the Vatican and the germ-infested river were perceived and predictable dangers, the scariest threats – because they are the least predictable – came from those unseen predators, in which elements of the unnatural or even the supernatural combined with physical fears to panic the populace. The monster scares which have from time to time arisen among the citizens of London provoked a variety of responses, depending on the prevailing cultural climate and the immediate circumstances; between them, they offer a fascinating insight into the diversity of collective behavior.

1711-1712 Scowerers and Mohocks

"Who has not heard the Scowerer's midnight fame ?
Who has not trembled at the Mohock's name ?"

So John Gay, author of *The Beggar's Opera*, wrote in 1712; and indeed, in that year all London had been thrown into panic by the Scowerers (= Scourers) and their successors the Mohocks (= Mohawks).

Street crime was nothing new in the streets of London. In 1598,

Street Gangs

Captain Bobadill, in Ben Jonson's *Every Man in His Humour*, speaks of "brave fellows indeed; in those days a man could not go from the Rose Tavern to the Piazza [in Covent Garden] once, but he must venture his life twice." During the following century, those who walked the streets had to beware of the Hectors, the Muns, and other street gangs, one rising to notoriety as another faded, just as with the gangs of our own day.

In 1712, however, the assaults of the Mohocks threatened to raise the customary level of street violence to new heights. Their favored activity was said to be "Tipping the Lion," a euphemism for crushing the noses of their victims and gouging out their eyes with the thumbs. "They slit the ears and distend the mouths with peculiar instruments of iron."[1]

> On the 6th of June 1712, Sir Mark Cole and three other gentlemen were tried at the Old Bailey for riot, assault and beating the watch. A paper of the day asserts that these were "Mohocks," that they had attacked the

watch in Devereux Street, slit two persons' noses, cut a woman in the arm with a penknife so as to disable her for life, rolled a woman in a tub down Snow Hill, misused other women in a barbarous manner by setting them on their heads, and overset several coaches and [sedan] chairs with short clubs, loaded with lead at both ends, expressly made for the purpose. In their defence the prisoners denied that they were Mohocks, alleging that they were "Scourers," and had gone out, with a magistrate's sanction, to scour the streets, arrest Mohocks and other offenders, and deliver them up to justice. On the night in question they had attacked a notorious gambling-house, and taken thirteen men out of it. While engaged in this meritorious manner, they learned that the Mohocks were in Devereux Street, and, on proceeding, found three men, desperately wounded, lying on the ground; they were then attacked by the watch, and felt bound to defend themselves. As an instance of the gross misconduct of the watch, it was further alleged that they, the watch, had on the same night actually presumed to arrest a peer of the realm, Lord Hitchinbroke, and had latterly adopted the practice of going their rounds by night accompanied by savage dogs. The jury, however, in spite of this defence, returned a verdict of guilty; and the judge fined the culprits in the sum of three shillings and fourpence each.[2]

Clearly the jury was not deceived by the devious attempt to lay the blame on others. John Bouch, the watchman, told how he had been threatened by a gang of twenty Mohocks who proposed to nail him in his watch-box and trundle him down the pavement; he had arrested three of the ringleaders and driven off the remainder with his sword. Gay, quoted above, refers to this incident and wrote a play, entitled *The Mohocks*, which was printed that year though apparently never performed.

Steele's *Spectator* refers to "the late panic fear" inspired by roaming bands of men, known as Mohocks, who attacked people in the street. The motive does not seem to have been robbery. Lady Wentworth declared that "they are said to be young gentlemen: they never take any money from any..."[3] Instead, what amused them was inflicting physical harm – disfiguring the men, sexually assaulting the women. Understandably, this so alarmed the populace that in 1712 a royal proclamation offered £100 – equivalent to nearly $20,000 today – for their apprehension.

The watchman incident seems to have been the climax of the Mohocks' reign of terror, for in March Jonathan Swift felt able to write in a letter to his friend Stella that "our Mohocks are all vanished." But if the Mohocks quit the scene, the stage was soon filled by other gangs. Some were out-and-out criminals, such as "Lady Holland's Mob," which terrorized Bartholomew Fair; others were clubs of aristocratic rakes such as the Hell-Fire Club, more interested in amusement (at the expense of others) than in mere crime.[4]

However, of all the London street gangs, it was the Mohocks who lived most vividly in the memory of Londoners. Nearly three centuries later they were still sufficiently remembered to inspire an episode of the classic television series *The Avengers* in which Steed and Mrs. Peel are confronted by a re-incarnation of the 18th century fiends, imitating the originals and even speaking what they supposed to be an 18th century style of speech.

1788-1790 The London Monster

Over a period of two years, ladies in central London – mostly young ladies – were subjected to attacks by male molesters. Such incidents occur in all cities, and street life in 18th century London was notoriously rough and violent. However, the assaults which were carried out during this period tended to be of a particular kind, leading to the supposition that they were the work of a single predator, who was unimaginatively nicknamed "The London Monster."

The incident considered the first of its kind took place in May 1788, when a young wife, Maria Smith, was approached in Fleet Street by a thin, short, ugly man wearing a cocked hat. He began talking to her in an indecent, eager way, talking and walking beside her till she reached her destination. When she asked him to stop

London Monster

following her, he grinned and made no reply. As she knocked on the door of the house she was visiting, he jumped onto the step beside her and struck her violently below the left breast and on the leg. Inside the house, it was found that she had been stabbed in the thigh with a sharp instrument like a lancet or a penknife, and only her corset had protected her from a similar wound to the chest. She was exceedingly disturbed by the attack, and later claimed that the shock confined her to her bed for many months, when her life was despaired of.

This attack set the pattern for the majority of the subsequent attacks, of which Jan Bondeson in *The London Monster* lists 55 in all, though he accepts that some of them may have been either imagined attacks or attention-seeking inventions. Most targeted single women walking in the streets, usually young, respectable and even elegant; occasionally groups of two or three would be threatened. The attack was generally initiated by obscene talk and indecent suggestions, and then the perpetrator would suddenly slash the victim, usually on the buttocks or thighs. There was never any serious attempt at rape or killing, but some of the wounds were quite severe. The fact that the attacks were generally similar supported the popular supposition that one person was responsible for all the attacks, and several of the descriptions seemed to bear this out.

By April 1789 there had been a sufficient number of these attacks for Londoners to feel seriously alarmed. The Bow Street Runners and others who formed the rudimentary police force of London at this date had no success in catching or even discouraging the monster. At a meeting in Lloyd's coffee house, a wealthy insurance broker, John Julius Angerstein, opened a subscription for a reward, and a group of gentlemen subscribed a total of £100 – a very considerable sum in those days, equivalent to some $16,000 in today's money. Posters announcing the reward were put up, and soon all London was hunting for the Monster. In the St. Pancras district, 15 gentlemen set up a nightly patrol between half an hour before sunset and 11 pm, and numerous other self-appointed vigilantes set out to win the reward.

Though Angerstein's intention had been to put Londoners on the alert, the effect was to increase the alarm of the female inhabitants. Rumors proliferated. Some thought the Monster to be an evil spirit who could make himself invisible to escape detection; others, that he was a master of disguise who could change his appearance at will. Another theory was that he was a mad nobleman who had vowed to maim every beauty in London – a theory discounted by the fact that some of the Monster's victims were less than beautiful. Any man was looked at with apprehension. The *Oracle* newspaper reported:

> It is really distressing to walk our streets towards evening. Every woman we meet regards us with distrust, shrinks sideling from our touch, and expects a poignard to pierce what gallantry and manhood consider as sacred.

Inevitably, one result was to bring about a spate of false identifications and even false arrests. Angerstein admitted that his reward had had no better result than that several innocent people had been accused, and sometimes beaten up by vigilantes before being dragged to the magistrates' office. He commented:

> It became dangerous for a man even to walk along the streets alone, as merely calling or pointing out some person as THE MONSTER, to the people passing, was sufficient to endanger his life; and many were robbed, and extremely abused, by this means. No man of gallantry dared to approach a lady in the streets after dark, for fear of alarming her susceptible nature. The whole order of things was changed. It was not safe for a gentleman to walk the streets, unless under the protection of a lady.

As always in such cases, anyone who behaved in any kind of suspicious manner was liable to be pointed out and even attacked. "One Monster-hunter arrested his employer after beating and pummelling him; another took his brother-in-law into custody and brought him to Bow Street. One lunatic arrested a butcher at gun point, after finding a bloody knife in his pocket."[5] A drunken naval lieutenant, whose coat matched a victim's description, was committed to Clerkenwell prison but soon discharged when his supposed victim, who shrieked when first confronted with him, subsequently admitted she couldn't be sure he was the man. Numerous such incidents took place.

The best way to avoid the Monster was, of course, to stay at home. For those unwilling to do so, however, protective measures were sought. It was reported that several ladies ordered underwear made from sheet copper to wear beneath their skirts. The less well off improvised more rudimentary armor with cardboard and the like.

Although most of the victims described their attacker in similar terms, many others did not. There can be little doubt that no one person was responsible for all the attacks, apart from the fact that in some cases more than one attacker was involved. Although most spoke of "the" monster, Angerstein's later poster declared that "there is great Reason to fear that more than ONE of these WRETCHES infest the streets." Criminals realized that the monster scare gave them unprecedented opportunities; a pickpocket had only to shout "The Monster!" to distract attention from his pilfering. And not all the supposed victims were what they seemed. A Miss Barrs, daughter of a fruiterer in Marylebone Street, gave a vivid account of how she had been attacked, but investigation revealed that she had cut her own clothes, and gave herself a cut in the calf, by way of making herself a celebrity.

One variant of the attacks was for the attacker to thrust a nosegay of real or artificial flowers in the lady's face, in which a sharp instrument was concealed, cutting her features. When a young Welshman named Rhynwick Williams was arrested on 13 June 1790, the fact that he was employed in a manufactory of artificial flowers was seen as damning, though the actual circumstances of his arrest were very dubious. His principal accuser, Anne Porter, identified him as the man who had made obscene talk to her and slashed her clothing, and it was true that Williams, a weak and less than admirable character, was in the habit of chatting up women in the street. This was not an unusual practice at the time, but there were other circumstantial reasons to suspect him. He admitted to knowing Miss Porter, by sight if nothing else. But he denied the attack, and produced a watertight alibi for the evening in question. Nevertheless he was arrested, tried, and convicted, and committed to Newgate where he was imprisoned for several years.

It is possible that Williams was responsible for some of the alleged attacks, but not a scrap of evidence showed this beyond a reasonable doubt. Apart from his alibi, the identification made by Anne Porter was doubtful and there was plenty of counter-evidence. Even if there was a single "monster" who set the pattern, no one villain could have carried out all the attacks. The fact that they ceased after Williams' arrest encouraged the public to think the Monster had been laid to rest, but it is equally likely that the arrest scared off those responsible for the attacks.

1803 – The "Hammersmith Ghost"

> There is no folly more predominant...than a ridiculous and superstitious fear of ghosts and apparitions...The inhabitants of the London suburb of Hammersmith were much alarmed by a nocturnal appearance which for a considerable time eluded detection or discovery. In the course of this unfortunate affair, two innocent persons met with an untimely death; and as the transaction engaged the attention of the public in a high degree, we shall fully relate the particulars of it.

Joseph Taylor's book on apparitions is a skeptical work, and the story of the Hammersmith Ghost confirmed his finding that "servants, nurses, old women, and others of the same standard of wisdom, to pass away the tediousness of a winter's evening, please and terrify themselves with strange relations, till they are even afraid of removing their eyes from one another, for fearing of seeing a *pale spectre* entering the room."[6]

In December 1803 rumors began to circulate in the London suburb of Hammersmith that a mysterious figure resembling a ghost had been seen in the lanes at night. Ghosts were commonly supposed to be revenants, spirits of the dead rising from the grave and returning to revisit the living, wearing the shrouds in which they had been buried. On 29 December the neighborhood watchman, William Girdle, saw the apparition. He chased after it; it fled, throwing off a sheet in the process, and got away.

The discarding of the sheet ought to have made it evident that this was no ghost, but a human impostor. But not every account

Hammersmith Ghost

could be so easily explained. Thomas Groom, a brewer's servant, told how he was walking through Hammersmith churchyard with a fellow servant when he was assaulted by something that clutched at his throat; yet he saw nothing. When others added such scary details as horns and glassy eyes, the notion spread that the figure was truly supernatural. A rumor was put about that it was the re-appearance of a man who had cut his throat in the neighborhood about a year before. From this point, the notion of a ghost from the grave was the prevailing belief.

Neither man, woman, or child would pass that way for some time, particularly after an event in January 1804 when a poor woman, far advanced in her pregnancy of a second child, was passing near the churchyard about two o'clock at night, when she beheld a figure rise from the tomb-stones. It was tall, and very white. She attempted to run, but the entity soon overtook her, and pressed her in its arms. She fainted, and her unconscious body was discovered by neighbors, who roused her and kindly led her home. She was so much shocked that she took to her bed, and two days later died as a consequence of her terror.

Several self-appointed vigilantes lay in wait on different nights, hoping to catch the ghost, but there were so many bye-lanes and paths leading to Hammersmith that it always managed to be in an unguarded way, and continued to "play his tricks" every night, to the terror of pedestrians. Nor were all the victims on foot; a wagoner was driving a team of eight horses when he was confronted by the figure. Though he was carrying sixteen passengers, he jumped to the ground and fled, leaving his wagon, horses, and passengers, to the mercies of the ghost.

On 3 January Francis Smith, an excise officer, determined to lie in wait for the apparition, armed with a gun, in Black Lion Lane. He must have thought luck had favored him when the supposed entity came in sight. He challenged him twice but received no reply, so he then fired at the figure, which fell. He told John Locke, a wine merchant, that he had shot the ghost – but it was found to be Thomas Milwood, a bricklayer, who wore white clothing as was customary in his occupation. Milwood had already alarmed people on more than one occasion and had been warned to cover up his white working clothes with a greatcoat. This he had neglected to do with fatal consequences. At the coroner's inquest, this rash act was judged willful murder, and Smith was accordingly committed to gaol. At the ensuing sessions at the Old Bailey, on 13 January, the jury at first found him guilty of manslaughter, but the crime being deemed murder in the eye of the law, the judge could only receive a verdict of Guilty or acquittal. He was consequently found guilty and was sentenced to be hanged in a few days' time, but was pardoned on condition of being imprisoned one year.[7]

There are no reports of the ghost being seen from that time on, and we may suppose that Milwood's tragic end discouraged the "ghost," who was never identified.

1837-1838 – Springheel Jack

In September 1837 three girls on Barnes Common, southwest London, reported a man in a dark cloak vaulting the railings of a churchyard. He tore their clothes then ran off laughing loudly. In October, a strange account was reported from nearby Streatham; the drivers of a coach told how their horses had been frightened by a huge creature, "whether man or bird or beast they could not say." Further reports of attack came in. On one occasion footprints were left that seemed to show the mysterious being had "machines or springs" on his shoes, and this led quickly to the mystery predator being dubbed "Springed-heel" or "Springheel Jack."

Further events followed in quick succession. On 11 October a barmaid attending Blackheath Fair was twice molested. On the first occasion her shawl was simply pulled from her shoulders, but later, as she was going home, a laughing man "who looked like a nobleman" bounded after her in great strides and ripped her clothes with what seemed to be iron claws. An observant girl, she couldn't help noticing that he was spitting blue flames; this, together with his fiery eyes and a smell of sulphur, caused her to faint.

Through the closing months of the year, similar reports spread throughout southwest London as far as Kingston. In February 1838, further away in Limehouse, Lucy Scales was pounced on by a tall, cloaked man who, again, spat blue flames at her. Nor was it only women in open places who were attacked. Jane Alsop in Bow opened her door to a man who claimed to be a police officer in chase of Springheel Jack, but who then attacked her, tearing at her clothing and hair until she was rescued by members of her family. "He was wearing a kind of helmet, and a tight-fitting white costume like an oilskin. His face was hideous, his eyes were like balls of fire. His hands had great claws, and he vomited blue and white flames." On another occasion, a maidservant who answered the door was confronted by a figure so terrifying that she took leave of her senses.

Though descriptions of the monster varied in detail, they generally conformed to the description of a tall, athletic figure, dressed in a long cloak and high-heeled boots. One mentioned a helmet, another a coat of mail. He had fiery eyes and claw-like fingers; some credited him with pointed ears. A servant girl in Forest Hill was scared into fits by a figure resembling a bear.

The attacks were frightening but seldom serious. There was no attempt at rape and no serious wounding. As with the London

Spingheel Jack

THE UNIVERSE WANTS TO PLAY

Monster, the intention seemed to be to cause a fright, to rip or slash clothing, and perhaps inflict superficial wounds.

Though all but a few of the incidents took place in southwest London, rumors proliferated throughout the city, and the number of attacks led to the Lord Mayor of London expressing his concern. Admiral Codrington organized a fund to offer a reward for the apprehension of Jack, personally contributing £100 – no small sum at the time. The fund eventually reached £1,000 but the reward was never claimed. Another eminent figure to take the menace seriously was the duke of Wellington. The victor of Waterloo, now in his sixties, set out on his horse several nights running, armed with pistols, but never caught sight of Jack.

Although many of the accounts pointed towards a supernatural being, opinion generally favored the idea that a human being was responsible. If so, the most eligible candidate was Henry de la Poer Beresford, marquis of Waterford, a wealthy 27-year old Irish peer, educated at Eton college, who indulged himself in travel, sport, and riotous living. He was notorious for wild escapades and cruel practical jokes, and for his readiness to bet on anything. It was assumed that he was performing the role of Springheeled Jack in consequence of such a bet. Two boys, whose mother was attacked in Clapham churchyard, described the attacker as a tall, slim young man wearing dark clothing and a cape and a hat. Brewer[8] takes it as certain that Waterford was to blame, and Haining has made out a very persuasive case for his responsibility, though the evidence is admittedly only circumstantial.[9] His character was certainly in keeping, and he is known to have been resident in London at the time of many of the incidents.

However, the sheer number of assaults means that no one person could possibly have been responsible for all of them. This may be because many were purely imaginary – as was almost certainly the case – or because Jack's deeds inspired copycat attacks. Though the original Springheel Jack was never caught or even positively identified, his exploits diminished in 1838 and the panic died down in consequence. But in 1845 a Mr. Purdy of Yarmouth, wandering delirious in his nightshirt, alarmed a neighbor who called for help; he was attacked by a young man on suspicion of being "Spring-heeled Jack," though his death was attributed to natural causes.[10] Occasional reports continued to be made long after there was any chance that Waterford could have been responsible. Thus Brewer reports that "even so late as 1877-8 an officer in her majesty's service caused much excitement at Aldershot, Colchester and elsewhere by his 'spring-heel' pranks. In Chichester and its neighbourhood the tales told of this adventure caused quite a little panic, and many people were afraid to venture out after sunset… I myself investigated some of the cases reported to me, but found them for the most part Fakenham ghost tales" [i.e. natural causes misinterpreted]. By this time Jack had become a folklore figure. Folklorist Jacqueline Simpson reports that in 1887 maids who had just received their wages were afraid to go out because "there are so many of these spring-heeled jacks about," and the name was used as a popular bogey to frighten naughty children.[11]

1856 and 1862 – The Garrotting Scares

> Garrotting came into practice in the early fifties, and was essentially a winter crime, favoured by the secrecy and the isolation of a London fog. The method is well known, and needs no detailed description. The thief approaches his victim from behind, and suddenly throws his arm round his neck, tightening the pressure even to suffocating point, when, strangulation being near, outcry is impossible. Other thieves – one or more – then turn out the pockets of the helpless prisoner. [12]

Street robbery was nothing new, of course, but garrotting was street robbery with a scary difference. Magazines of the day described the method as an attack from behind, bringing the arm under the victim's throat across the Adam's apple, cutting off the air till the victim was unconscious, rendering him powerless to resist and leaving him on the ground writhing in agony, "with tongue protruding and eyes starting from their sockets."[13]

Crime statistics are notoriously difficult to establish, partly because of uncertain definition, partly because crimes reported are not necessarily equivalent to crimes committed. However, after studying the statistics, Sindall has concluded not only that the streets of Victorian London were substantially safer than those of neo-Elizabethan London, but that they did not become significantly more dangerous during the period of the garrotting scares. In other words, it was the perception of danger, not the danger itself, which caused the panic. In November 1856 the London *Times* editorialized that there existed parts of London "inhabited by a numerous and respectable population" where a man cannot walk "without imminent danger of being throttled, robbed, and if not actually murdered, at least kicked and pommelled within an inch of his life."[14] That winter that newspaper published no less than seven editorials and 31 letters on the subject, many calling for extreme legal action such as the reinstatement of hanging for the offence. The judges responded to the popular feeling, and sentences became heavier; in November 1856 two garrotters were transported for life.

The garrotting panics first escalated in 1856, then subsided in the following spring and during 1857, only to burst out anew in July 1862. This second wave of panic was triggered by an attack on a Member of Parliament, Mr. Pilkington, returning at 1 am after a late sitting along Pall Mall, one of the most respectable streets of London. (The attack achieved literary fame when Trollope borrowed it for his political novel *Phineas Finn*.) Seemingly, the number of garrotting assaults rapidly increased, but this may simply have been due to press coverage and/or an increase in police activity in response to public demand.

Unlike the exploits of the Hammersmith Ghost and Springheel Jack, the garrotters were never thought to be anything but real flesh-and-blood criminals. In 1862, 27 offenders of this class were arraigned at one and the same time at the Central Criminal Court. Very heavy sentences were imposed on all, and the crime was scotched for a time, though not entirely killed. Judges had the power of imposing flogging, and this acted as a powerful deterrent. But not so powerful as to stop garrotting altogether; in 1895-6 a gang led by a man named Smith, known as "the countryman," carried out some fifty attacks in two months in the Borough, London. He eventually shot himself when cornered by the police after a robbery.

Although Griffiths describes garrotting as "a winter crime"

Garrotters

performed under cover of darkness or fog, many attacks took place in broad daylight. "One gentleman was garrotted in the afternoon near Paternoster Row, another in Holborn, a third in Cockspur Street," three busy streets with plenty of passers-by. "A young lady of 15 was attacked in Westbourne Crescent about 4 pm. While she was half-throttled the thieves tore off her necklace and dragged the pendants from her ears. They had meant to cut off her hair, which was long and fine, and worth a considerable sum, but just then the ruffians were frightened from their prey."

Though the garrotters were a genuine menace, the alarm they aroused in the minds of Londoners was out of all proportion to the real danger. Anti-garrotting devices were on sale to protect the victim and injure the attacker, including spiked collars such as are worn by some dogs.

One feature of the scares was that they were perceived as essentially an attack on the middle class. It is not surprising that the satirical journal *Punch*, quintessentially a middle-class publication, dedicated much of its coverage to the garrotting menace during this period, for example making absurd suggestions for protective devices. Another noteworthy aspect is that though the garrotting scare was felt to be peculiar to London, in fact the pedestrian in either Liverpool or Manchester was in relatively much greater danger. But the *Daily News* was referring to London when it spoke of "a lair of footpads and assassins by night."

By the 1860s, the popular press was greatly more accessible to the general public than it had been in the time of the London Monster or Springheel Jack, and the garrotting scare not only spread by word of mouth but was fueled by the newspaper coverage. Significantly, though the image of the garrotter became a symbol of popular terror, no one individual or group was singled out, with the consequence that the menace remained shadowy and undefined. This was because, though a number of attacks undoubtedly took place, the panic was disproportionate to the reality, inflated by exaggerated press reports.

1888 – The Whitechapel Murders

The series of five murders that took place over a three-month period, August-November 1888, gave rise to the biggest panic of its kind ever experienced by Londoners, rousing an interest that has scarcely died down after more than a century. The horrific nature of the killings, the fact that we have detailed knowledge of the circumstances, combined with the fact that the killer was never caught or even positively identified, not only defied the best efforts of a very competent police force at the time, but has been a challenge ever since to countless investigators and armchair theorists.

All five victims were, if not professional prostitutes, at best women of loose repute. The first victim in the series, on 31 August, was 43-year-old Mary Ann "Polly" Nichols. A newspaper report the following morning asserted that "no murder was ever more ferociously and more brutally done." The second, on 8 September, was "Dark Annie" Chapman, aged 47. On 30 September two more were killed "Long Liz" Stride, aged 45, and Catherine Eddowes, aged 46. The first four were killed in the street, but the fifth, Mary Jane Kelly, at 25 the youngest of the victims, was killed indoors. With this killing the spate of murders stopped, a fact that has only added to the mystery.

However, popular concern extended the catalogue. Previous to the Nichols murder there had been three killings, of "Fairy Fay" in 1887, Emma Smith and Martha Turner in 1888; and after Kelly there were two more – Anne McKenzie in 1889 and Frances Coles in 1891. None of these is now considered to be a victim of the same killer, but at the time it seemed logical to the terrified populace to chalk up their names to the same assassin's score.

All the murders took place at night in a geographically limited area, the Whitechapel district of London, then a rough and squalid quarter. All were extremely brutal, yet painstakingly carried out with savage yet precise mutilation. Kelly, for instance, was nearly beheaded by a cut to her throat; her abdomen was partially ripped open, across and downwards, the entrails wrenched away and removed, but the liver excised and placed between the feet; one of her hands was placed inside her stomach; both breasts were severed from the body; the left arm was nearly amputated; and the nose had been cut off, the forehead skinned, the thighs and calves stripped of flesh. While such savagery suggested insanity, it also indicated a considerable degree of surgical skill; from the start the investigators were looking for a man with medical experience.

Whitechapel

LONDON'S MONSTER SCARES   93

The horrific circumstances produced an intense public reaction. Already, by the second killing, the public – encouraged by the press – had become fascinated by the case. The *Penny Illustrated Paper* reported that a large crowd had congregated at the site of Chapman's murder; neighbors were charging spectators to inspect the scene from their windows. Inevitably, this interest led to a spate of rumors. A huge array of suspects were considered, ranging from the eminent surgeon Sir William Gull to the Duke of Clarence, by way of the painter Walter Sickert and the poet James Kenneth Stephen. The famous philanthropist Dr. Barnardo, who performed good works in the district, also came under suspicion; he had been seen talking with the victim Stride four days before she was killed. Such circumstantial evidence made it possible to draw up a plausible case against each of these people, but none was ultimately convincing and despite a great deal of police activity, none was ever arraigned.

Apart from these celebrity suspects, a string of dubious characters were taken into custody, and some actually charged; but each in turn was released as the evidence proved insufficient. For example, a man named Pizer had been seen speaking with Chapman shortly before her death; moreover he was a leather-worker who used sharp-bladed knives in his profession. But he had a solid alibi for Nichols' murder, and his appearance was quite at variance with the description of Chapman's killer given by possible witnesses.

In September 1888, a letter was delivered at the Central News Agency, addressed to "The Boss." It purported to be from the killer and went into some detail about the murders. "I am down on whores and shant quit ripping them till I do get buckled" [caught]. However, the letter is not generally considered genuine and is suspected to be the handiwork of a journalist intent on building up a sensational story. If so, it certainly succeeded, for it was signed "Jack the Ripper" – a name that was immediately seized on by the public and which has stuck to the case ever since.

After the double event of 30 September, morbid interest turned to panic. That the killer should strike twice in one night, when the whole district was on the lookout for him, showed that Londoners were challenged by someone who combined an almost reckless fearlessness with his other qualities – qualities which included an intimate knowledge of the labyrinthine alleys and courtyards of the district, sufficient familiarity with the local population to select his victims with care, and a horrifying degree of medical expertise combined with the callousness required first to attack the victims with such savagery and then subject their corpses to such macabre mutilations. Nothing less than a monster, it was thought, could carry out such calculated assaults.

Indeed, some theorists, focusing on the frenzied character of the killings, looked to a real monster: a baboon, such as the one featured in Poe's "The Murders in the Rue Morgue" tale, was proposed. Others concentrated on the question of motivation. There were those – author Conan Doyle among them – who suspected a woman, avenging the death of her sister who had been enticed into prostitution and died. The large Jewish population of the area combined with the meticulous mutilation led others to suspect Judaic ritual slaughter. Then and later there were false confessions that had to be followed up before being rejected. Both at the time, and ever since, a prodigious quantity of surmise and supposition was created but leading to no satisfactory conclusion.

Public interest and alarm were greater than with any of the previous London "monsters." At the height of the panic, more than a thousand letters every week were addressed to the police, offering advice and suggestions for catching the killer. The careful selection of the victims meant that others living outside the monster's killing ground could feel relatively safe – except that the simple knowledge that such a fiend was at work in the London streets was cause for alarm. In face of the police failure to catch the killer, self-appointed vigilante groups patrolled the streets. Letters to the press targeted police inefficiency – quite unjustifiably, as the police effort was massive: 80,000 leaflets distributed to local residents, house-to-house questioning, searches by plain clothed policemen, and policewomen working undercover. The panic died down only with the fifth killing, and even then was liable to start up again with a fresh incident, even if clearly not by the same hand. For the monster was never caught.

The Pattern of Terror
Considered as a group and in retrospect, we can see that diverse

though these several events were in many ways, they shared a common denominator: *fear*. Each of the "monsters" became some kind of bogeyman, reflecting and embodying the latent terrors of the Londoner.

They differed from traditional folklore bogies – witches, demons – by the fact that their exploits were flesh-and-blood crimes performed by flesh-and-blood perpetrators. Yet the popular imagination endowed them with larger-than-life features – Springheel Jack was widely believed to be a supernatural being, the Hammersmith Ghost was one by definition, the London Monster was thought by some to be an evil spirit. Even when the crimes were all too human – the Mohocks, the garrotters – the predators acquired a superhuman dimension by what they did and how they did it, while the horrific character of the Ripper's killings made him seem less than human.

Looking for patterns, we note at once that the predators were all male, the victims in most cases female, though the Mohocks and Garrotters also attacked males for the purpose of mutilation or robbery. Consequently it can reasonably be supposed that the primary motivation involved some degree of sexual perversion. This is confirmed by the nature of the attacks, targeting thighs and buttocks in the less serious cases, involving sadistic murder in the more serious ones.

Since, though some arrests were made, none of the London monsters was ever convincingly caught, psychiatric evaluation of the motivation involved has to be a matter of speculation. However, some light is thrown by cases elsewhere which afforded greater opportunity for study. Bondeson has pointed to a number of parallel occurrences in other countries.[16] The streets of Paris in 1819 were infested with *piqueurs* who attacked women in the buttocks or thighs with sharp instruments, customarily rapiers attached to canes or umbrellas. The attacks were very like those of the London Monster and may have been carried out in imitation of them. Here too there was widespread public alarm, vigilantes, offer of rewards, and a similar dying down of the scare after an individual had been arrested – though, as with Williams in London, with considerable doubts that he was really the person responsible. At Bozen, Germany, there was a similar outbreak by a so-called *Madchenstecher* (girl-stabber) in 1828-9, where a soldier confessed; another at Leipzig in the 1860s, Strasbourg and Bremen in 1880, Mainz in 1890. In the United States in the 1890s, a serial attacker nicknamed "Jack the Cutter" was active in Brooklyn attacking women, and in 1906 "Jack the Stabber" in St Louis was similarly occupied until his capture.

In 1819, the same year as the Paris outbreak, a similar wave of assaults on women took place in Augsburg, Germany. Here again some kind of copycat procedure can be supposed. Remarkably, 18 years later a man named Carl Bartle was finally arrested and confessed to being the *madchenschneider* (girl-cutter). Since the man was clearly mentally disturbed, he was subjected to a medico-legal examination. He explained that he had always been obsessed by the sight of blood; his first attack, carried out when he was 19, had given him intense pleasure culminating in ejaculation.

It is fair to conclude that sexual perversion, amounting in some instances to sadism, underlaid all the London monster attacks. What takes them out of the department of individual psychology and into the sociologist's field of interest is that each in turn triggered a public response that perceived the attackers, not as deranged individuals, but as larger-than-life creations.

The tendency of the populace was, wherever possible, to designate *a single monster.* In fact, it is certain that the incidents attributed to the London Monster or Springheel Jack could not all have been carried out by a single perpetrator. Even if there was indeed an individual who initiated the series, he was soon followed by copycats who deliberately sought, or were psychologically driven, to emulate his deeds. This tendency was most marked in the case of the Whitechapel murders where, though five of the killings were almost certainly the work of a single serial killer, popular alarm created a folklore figure which after a hundred years has not lost its appeal. Thus Peter Sutcliffe, a 20th century serial killer who confessed to 13 killings between 1975-1981, was named "the Yorkshire Ripper" in deliberate evocation of his 19th century predecessor; he, too, targeted prostitutes, claiming to have received a mandate from God to destroy them.

So we find that, in contrast to many of the urban panics recorded in the history of London and other cities, the issues in these monster-scares were neither political, nor religious, nor related to public health or other community issues. Instead, they had their roots in human pathology and, perhaps for that reason, awoke an atavistic fear in the populace, endowing them with a monstrous significance.

NOTES

[1] Fuller, Ronald. *Hell-fire Francis*. London: Chatto & Windus, 1939: 18

[2] *Chambers Book of Days*, volume 1, page 743

[3] Quoted from the Wentworth Papers on wikipedia.org/wiki/Mohocks

[4] Fuller, 22

[5] Bondeson, Jan. *The London Monster*. London: Free Association, 2000: 35

[6] Taylor, Joseph. *Apparitions, or the Mystery of Ghosts*. London: Lackington, Alle 1815: 156

[7] The Newgate Calendar

[8] Brewer, E. Cobham. *The Reader's Handbook*. London: Chatto & Windus [revised edition], 1925: 192

[9] Haining, Peter. *The Legend and Bizarre Crimes of Spring Heeled Jack*. London: Frederick Muller, 1977.

[10] *Illustrated London News*, 27 September 1845

[11] Jacqueline Simpson, "Spring-Heeled Jack," *Foaftale News* 48, January 2001

[12] Griffiths, Major Arthur. *Mysteries of Police and Crime*. London circa 1900: volume 3: 230

[13] R. Sindall, "The London Garotting [sic] Panics of 1856 and 1862," *Social History* 12.3. 351 (1987) 351

[14] Sindall, 352

[15] Bondeson, 176+

ACKNOWLEDGMENTS: The photos accompanying this article were provided courtesy of the Mary Evans Picture Library. For more information, see www.maryevans.com.

HILARY EVANS and **ROBERT BARTHOLOMEW** are the authors of *Panic Attacks: Media Manipulation and Mass Delusion*. This article is adapted from an entry in their yet to be published *Encyclopedia of Exceptional Social Behavior*, a comprehensive survey of episodes of moral panic, collective enthusiasm, communal fears and "mass hysteria," ranging from the Children's Crusades of the Middle Ages to the suicide bombers of the 21st Century. Underlying their project is the hope that, by noting similarities and tracing patterns, we may gain a deeper understanding of what motivates and triggers such outbreaks and directs their course.

THE BIO-PHILES:
THOUGHTS OF A FORTEAN NATURALIST
By David Hricenak

Anomalistics and natural history have a great deal in common. Before I elaborate on that statement some definitions may be in order. Anomalistics is, of course, the study of all those phenomena that don't fit into the worldview of mainstream science, Fortean phenomena in other words. Natural history can be defined as the study of living things, usually pursued in the field rather than the lab. These days professional naturalists are more likely to call themselves ecologists or field biologists.

So what do these fields have in common? First of all is a certain lack of respect. The disdain of establishment science is something with which all anomalists are familiar. Naturalists don't have it quite so bad. They can still get published in refereed journals. But in the age of DNA people who study live organisms rather than their constituent molecules are increasingly seen as quaint and irrelevant.

A second similarity follows from the first. Any discipline that professionals avoid is wide open to amateurs. Please note that the word "amateur" does not necessarily mean sloppy or careless. Amateur anomalists and naturalists can and have made countless contributions to human knowledge.

A third similarity follows directly from number two and has a lot to do with number one. I'm talking about the importance of anecdotal data. Scientists are properly leery of eyewitness testimony. But both anomalists and naturalists know that interesting things don't always happen in front of a trained observer.

Finally there is a lot of overlap between these two disciplines. The books of Charles Fort and contemporary Fortean journals are full of anomalous observations involving animals, plants, fungi, and microbes. Researchers such as Karl Shuker and the late Ivan Sanderson have distinguished themselves as both naturalists and anomalists.

In the following four essays I explore this region of overlap. In the first I touch on the most prominent field of Fortean natural history and show what cryptozoologists may be missing by focusing on only one kingdom of life. In the second I go where even cryptozoologists fear to tread and speculate on what may be living over our heads. In the third I go even farther, into outer space, where some of our stranger life forms may have originated. And in the last I come back to Earth to discuss another favorite Fortean phenomenon, those creatures that persist in turning up where they aren't supposed to exist.

Cryptobotany

Cryptozoology is defined as the science of "hidden" animals. This discipline exists on the fringe of scientific respectability along with other protosciences like ufology and parapsychology. Of course, mainstream science has no problem with the concept of unknown species. After all, novelties turn up all the time and not just rain forest beetles. For example in the past decade several new kinds of hoofed mammals have been found in Southeast Asia and a new whale was just described last year.

The problem is methodology. Cryptozoologists mostly deal with anecdotal evidence such as folktales and eyewitness accounts. There is also a certain bias toward the spectacular and "monstrous." Of course this is no reason to dismiss the subject. Mythical monsters do sometimes turn out to be real. Consider the gorilla and the giant squid.

My only complaint involves the limits implied by calling the field crypto"zoo"ology. Why limit our studies to animals? What about the other kingdoms of life? Plants for instance.

Our first botanical cryptid comes from the island of Madagascar off the east coast of Africa. Madagascar is well known for its unusual animals, including lemurs, hedgehog-like tenrecs, and two-thirds of the world's chameleon species. Madagascar's plants are less well known but equally weird. Probably the weirdest of the known flora are the *Diddiereaceae*, a family of cactus-like succulents found nowhere else on Earth.

If we are to believe a nineteenth century German explorer

named Carle Liche , something even stranger grows on this peculiar island. I'm talking about a man-eating tree. Liche reported that the tree resembled an eight-foot tall pineapple, with eight large leaves hanging from the top, which also sprouted writhing snake-like tendrils. The plant also oozed an intoxicating liquid.

Liche further claimed to have witnessed a primitive tribeswoman being sacrificed to this botanical horror. The woman was forced to climb the tree and drink the fluid. At this point the tendrils wrapped around her body and the leaves rose up and crushed her. A few days later the leaves had flopped down to their normal position and all that was left of the woman was bones.

I realize the whole story sounds like something from a very bad horror movie. If Liche had been writing today instead of in 1878, the only periodical that would have published his account would be the *Weekly World News.* So far as I know no other Westerner has ever reported seeing this plant, although one Salmon Osborn searched for it during the 1920s.

Could such a creature even exist? What would it have fed on before humans arrived on Madagascar? Maybe the gorilla-sized lemurs that once roamed the island. Maybe the species almost went extinct when its prey did. Maybe Liche's tribespeople were conservationists, caring for the last specimen. Maybe I'm getting carried away.

Anyway there are also accounts of oversize carnivorous plants from Central and South America, none of which are represented in herbaria or botanical gardens. Their actual existence is highly unlikely, of course, but no more so than Bigfoot or the Loch Ness Monster.

Even deadlier and less likely are trees called the *upas* in Asia and the *umdhlebi* in Africa. Both of these trees are said to give off an airborne poison that kills anything that gets too close. The ground around the *upas* is said to be littered with the bones of its victims, human and animal. As for the *umdhlebi*, the only antidote for its poison is, ironically enough, the tree's fruit. Collecting it involves approaching the upwind side of the tree and hoping the wind doesn't shift.

So what can we make of all this? Actually, chemical warfare is quite common in the plant kingdom. Black walnut trees and creosote bushes release herbicides into the soil to kill competitors and many species produce toxins to discourage herbivores. Even airborne poisons are not completely unknown. For example, the common dandelion releases ethylene gas. But I'm not aware of any known example on the scale of our killer trees.

But, believe it or not, there may be some substance to these African tales. Several African lakes are known to "turn over," releasing catastrophic amounts of carbon dioxide gas and asphyxiating anyone nearby. An "event" at Lake Nyos in Cameroon in 1986 killed over 1,700 people and uncounted animals. It isn't hard to imagine someone coming across the aftermath of such an event and jumping to conclusions about the local flora. Interestingly enough there is also a valley in Java with a history of lethal carbon dioxide emissions. The local name for the place is Guwo Upas.

Not every botanical mystery is quite this lethal. Consider silphium. This was the ancient Roman name for a popular vegetable that apparently came from North Africa. Several classical authors mention it, and it also appears on sculptures. The mystery is that no modern botanist has ever found a plant matching the description of silphium. Perhaps the Romans ate it into extinction.

I think all of these examples prove that cryptobotany is as valid a subject as cryptozoology. There are also plenty of mysteries involving fungi and microbes. My modest proposal is that we rename the field cryptobiology. After all, why should the zoologists have all the fun?

What's Living Up There?

One running theme in the scientific news of the past few years is the continuous discovery of life thriving in ever less likely places. Researchers have found bacteria in rocks three miles down and whole living communities existing around deep-sea volcanic vents. Here at the surface, there doesn't seem to be anyplace too hot, cold, dry, or polluted for some form of life.

But there is one major habitat that life hasn't quite conquered yet. Every ecological community we know about is tied to the Earth's surface or its bodies of water. So far as we know nothing actually lives in the atmosphere.

There is always life up there of course. Birds, bats, and bugs fly and many other animals glide. And a whole host of little things ride the wind – bacteria, seeds and spores of all sorts, baby spiders on silken parachutes. The sky can be like an interstate on Thanksgiving weekend. But like the highway, everyone is on the way somewhere else. All of these organisms have to come to earth at some point in their lives.

Therein lies the puzzle. For all its transient nature, aerial plankton can be amazingly abundant. Ever since the 1930's people have towed nets behind aircraft and sampled this abundance. It has been estimated that a single cubic mile of atmosphere may hold 25 million airborne insects. The corresponding figures for bacteria, spores, *et al*, I will leave as an exercise for the reader.

Now oceanic plankton supports everything from sardines to blue whales but what feeds on the aerial stuff? Not much, it seems. Where high mountains thrust into the atmosphere, there are spiders and beetles that live on the fallout. And at lower elevations birds like swallows and swifts eat aerial insects. But that's about it. Where are the aerial whales? There is a major niche to fill here and nature is usually very good at filling niches. What happened?

Gravity is part of the problem. Air is not nearly as dense as water. How would these aerial whales stay aloft? I could imagine something like an organic dirigible evolving. After all, jellyfish use gasbags to sail over the ocean surface. But it hasn't actually happened. Or has it?

Ever since Kenneth Arnold's famous sighting in 1947 a number of people, including Arnold himself, have wondered whether UFOs might be an unrecognized atmospheric life form. One of the most vocal was a merchant marine radio officer named Trevor James Constable. In 1978 Constable wrote a book entitled *Sky Creatures*. He speculated that UFOs, which he called "critters," were actually huge single-celled organisms. These aren't often seen, according to Constable, because they are usually only visible in infrared light. His book was illustrated with infrared photos that look very biological. More recently there has been a great deal of speculation on the internet about peculiar organic-looking atmospheric objects called "Roswell rods," which apparently move too fast to be seen, but show up on video.

Okay, let's say that there are creatures flying around up there that we don't normally see. Presumably, like all living things, they eventually die. And logically dying should remove their means of support. In other words dead critters or rods should fall to Earth. Is there any evidence that they have?

Believe it or not, there may be. There is a long history of people seeing "meteors" and finding jelly-like material at the fall site. Welsh folklore even has a name for this substance – *pwdre se* – which roughly translates as "star rot." Unfortunately the stuff is said to dissolve quickly, and the few purported samples that have been analyzed turned out to be slime molds or algae.

There may also be a connection to ball lightning, the "foo-fighters" of World War II, and those mysterious localized entities often known as spook or ghost lights, all of which display behaviors indicating at least an animal level of intelligence. Physicists have never been able to explain any of those phenomena.

Maybe biologists should give it a shot.

Life From Elsewhere?

The late Terrance McKenna was one of a growing breed of ethnobotanists interested in how indigenous people make use of the plants and fungi in their environments. McKenna's interests were more than academic, however. He actually participated in the religious rituals of the Amazonian natives that he studied.

McKenna also believed that hallucinogenic mushrooms are an alien intelligence sent to Earth to enlighten the human race. This insight was acquired by ingesting hallucinogenic mushrooms. McKenna never explained how such intelligence could exist in an organism without a nervous system, though.

I'm not really trying to poke fun at Terrance McKenna, especially since he is no longer around to defend his ideas. Actually his speculations are part of a noble intellectual tradition, the idea that life on Earth, or at least some portion of it, is so strange and wonderful that it must have originated elsewhere.

Applied to life as a whole the idea has had some heavyweight defenders, including Francis Crick, co-discoverer of the structure of DNA, and maverick astronomer Sir Fred Hoyle. Both have devoted entire books to the concept.

In *Life Itself* Crick proposes that Earth was seeded by extraterrestrial intelligences in the distant past as part of a program to spread life throughout the Universe. In *Lifecloud* and *Diseases From Space* Hoyle and coauthor N. C. Wickramasinghe argue that outer space literally swarms with bacteria and viruses which occasionally rain down on Earth. This is supposedly how life began in the past and why epidemics spread so quickly today.

The individual species most commonly proposed as an ET is of course *Homo sapiens*. Many writers have felt that we humans are too different to have arisen here naturally. Erich van Daniken comes to mind, of course, but he has many ancestors and successors, most recently those cloning pioneers, the Raelians. I won't go into the "evidence" for our extraterrestrial origins here. Let's just say that properly interpreted myth can prove just about anything.

Another possible interstellar immigrant is the Venus' flytrap. You've probably seen these plants in your local garden center; they're usually sold in a little pot with a plastic cover. If you're like me you may have even bought one, taken it home, fed it some flies, and watched it die.

Mark Chorvinsky made the case for the flytrap's alien status in issue 12 of *Strange Magazine*. First of all, consider the trapping mechanism itself. A flytrap leaf is shaped like an open book with three sensitive hairs growing inside it. Touching one hair causes no reaction. But if two hairs are touched in succession the trap quickly closes. This cuts down on "false alarms." Moreover if an insect is small enough to escape, the trap quickly reopens without secreting any digestive enzymes. There are hundreds of species of insectivorous plants but none that use anything nearly as sophisticated.

Also, despite their abundance in plant stores, wild flytraps are only found in a narrow strip of coastal plain in North and South Carolina. And in the same area there is a series of peculiar round lakes called the Carolina Bays, the apparent product of an ancient meteorite bombardment. Chorvinsky suggests that the plants could have come to Earth with the meteors.

Well, maybe. The main problem I have with this idea is that I don't see how the flytraps could have survived the trip. These are specialized and not very hardy plants; they are not really suited to the rigors of space travel.

That objection, at least, doesn't apply to our next candidate. Rotifers are odd little animals common in most freshwater habitats. I first saw one in my high school biology class. We were supposed to be looking for *Paramecium,* the slipper-shaped protozoan you may dimly remember from your own school days. What I saw was a vaguely wormlike creature that had what looked like a tiny conveyer belt running at its front end. This was the animal's feeding apparatus and the source of the name rotifer, meaning "wheel-bearer." I was probably the only student in the class who knew what it was, or cared.

Anyway, like a lot of freshwater inhabitants, rotifers have a problem. Ponds tend to dry up. So many species can produce a special resting stage that is very resistant to cold and dryness and is also light enough to travel on the wind. This, and the fact that rotifers are so weird anatomically that zoologists can't agree on how to classify them, led biologist Lyall Watson to propose, in his book *Supernature,* that rotifer spores may have drifted to Earth from somewhere else, eventually proliferating into the two thousand known species.

Again, maybe. As a former biology major I have two main objections to most of these speculations. First of all, every creature I've mentioned, and every other plant, animal, or microbe ever studied, share the same genetic code. Second, Venus' flytraps, rotifers, and McKenna's mushrooms are all well adapted members of their respective ecosystems. They fit in too well to be aliens. When Earthly species are moved to a new habitat, they either die out or undergo a population explosion. They hardly ever just become well-adjusted citizens.

Which brings us back to *Homo sapiens.* We are not a well-adjusted species and we don't seem to really fit into any ecosystem. So maybe we are aliens after all.

Out Of Place

Until recently, I lived in a community called Birchwood Lakes in Pike County, Pennsylvania. Some time ago I was walking around one of the lakes that give the community its name and saw what looked like an unusual fungus of some sort. Always one to check out any kind of unusual growth, I investigated. It turned out to be a sizable chunk of coral, more likely something called clubbed finger coral (*Porites porites*), at least according to my Audubon Field Guide. So what, you ask? Let me repeat, I live in the northeast corner of Pennsylvania – not exactly reef country.

It's not the first time something like this has happened, either. When I was but a lad my uncle had a pond that he stocked with bullhead catfish. Not for fishing, mind you. These were more like poor man's koi. The high point of every visit was watching my uncle feed them dry dog chow. Anyway, on one of these visits I found a shell by the pond. Not a freshwater snail or mussel, either, but more like a small conch. Again, bear in mind this was northeastern Pennsylvania.

Okay, two incidents in forty-odd years don't prove anything. If I have some kind of wild talent for finding out-of-place marine specimens, it's pretty erratic. Both were recent specimens, not fossils, and they came from somewhere else. It's probably best to just assume someone dropped them and get on with our lives.

Of course, I'm not going to do that. Living things or their remains are always turning up where they shouldn't be. That scientific gadfly, Charles Fort, devoted his book *Lo!* to people, animals and things disappearing and appearing, coining the word "teleportation" as a possible explanation. And Forteans are still collecting such accounts today.

Of course, the stories that get published are usually more spectacular than a single shell by a pond – large wild cats roaming England, for example. The British Isles do have a species of wild cat (*Felis sylvestris*), but it's basically just an untamed tabby and is only supposed to be found in the Scottish highlands. The animals being seen and photographed, and sometimes killing, small livestock are usually identified as "panthers" or "pumas." Neither species is native to the British Isles.

In this country we do have pumas, at least. It's one of the many pseudonyms of *Felis concolor*. They're supposed to be extinct here in the northeast, but who knows? There are certainly plenty of deer for them to eat. What we don't have are kangaroos. Our only native marsupial is the opossum. Yet people in the Midwest have reported seeing kangaroos for years. In a 1974 incident, two Chicago cops even tried to put the cuffs on one.

So what exactly is going on here? The Brits might be seeing stray housecats and panicking, but it's hard to see what we Americans could be mistaking for kangaroos. The common sense interpretation is that we're dealing with escapes from zoos or private collections. No one ever comes forward, but if you had "misplaced" a potentially dangerous animal, would you?

Like I said, that's common sense. But how many people really lose cougars and kangaroos? There's also the mass panic theory, but "figments of the imagination" don't leave tracks and kill livestock. I know we've come a long way from a piece of coral by a lake, but maybe it all ties together somehow.

Let's get back to Charles Fort and teleportation. Fort was pretty vague about this but basically he was speculating about an unrecognized force moving stuff around in order to maintain the cosmic balance. So maybe, for some reason, the Midwest needs kangaroos, and it gets them.

Well, I said it was vague. I don't foresee a major research effort any time soon. (Although, considering what does get funded, who knows?) If something other than normal human absent-mindedness is going on, it would be nice to know about it. The first step would be collecting case histories, most of which are probably mundane, more like my coral than the Chicago kangaroo. With enough cases a pattern may emerge. That's how science works.

This is one case where we amateurs can make a contribution. Maybe there's nothing unusual happening after all. But we won't know until we check it out.

DAVID HRICENAK majored in biology from Wilkes College (now Wilkes University) in Wilkes-Barre PA. He wrote for the *INFO Journal* back the late 1970s and early 1980s and more recently a few nature articles for a local monthly newspaper in Milford, Pennsylvania. He is currently writing and pursuing a teaching career in Nashville, Tennessee.

THE HOBBITS OF FLORES
SCIENCE MEETS CRYPTOZOOLOGY
By Dwight G. Smith and Gary Mangiacopra

Up the airy mountain
Down the rushy glen
We daren't go a-hunting
For fear of little men.
– William Allingham

Peoples of every region of the globe have a treasure-trove catalog of superstitions, myths, legends, and folklore of little peoples. Sometimes these little people take the form of miniature humans, at other times they are transformed into little demons, elves, fairies, gnomes, and the like. Local names and traditions about these little people undoubtedly reflect the personalities of the people that derived and perpetrated the legends and associated traditions about each of the celebrated little people. Some little people were revered as benevolent; others were feared to be malevolent. Many were thought to possess magical powers.

The islanders of Flores told of a long-ago tribe of little people that inhabited the rain forest of their island. Said to be scarcely three feet tall, these little people walked upright like humans but spoke only in whispers and were renown for their voracious appetite. They were called *ebu gogo,* which translates as the "grandmother who eats everything." Westerners thought that possibly these were tales of macaques, which eat wild and cultivated fruits and grains as well as small animals. Even so, this hardly qualifies macaques as the grandmother who eats everything.

Native superstitions translated into hard science in September 2004, when a team of archaeologists from Australia and Indonesia discovered fossils of miniature humans in a cave on the island of

Flores. The discovery elevated tales of little people from the pages of cryptozoology books into articles in nationally recognized science journals.

First fossil finds included a nearly complete skeleton of an adult female and skeletal fragments of another individual. Later excavations within the cave obtained skeletal remains of an additional 5 individuals. The discovery team quickly concluded that the fossils represented an entirely new hominid species *Homo floresiensis*, thus setting it apart from our own species, *Homo sapiens*. The scientific diagnosis of this new species is, in part: small bodied bipedal hominid about one meter in body height with a cranial volume estimated at 380 square centimeters. Because of their small stature and grapefruit-sized brains the new hominid was quickly dubbed the "hobbit" in both popular and scientific literature.

Also associated with the hobbit fossils were the remains of fish, frogs, snakes, turtles, birds, and small rodents that were presumed to represent food remains. To many, the variety of animal remains with the fossils seemed to echo their native nickname as "the grandmother that eats everything." Although the hobbits were but a fraction of the size of modern humans, they manufactured rudimentary but sufficiently sophisticated tools such as large blades, awls, and possibly smaller, finely worked spear points. These tools coupled with the fact that they were able to hunt large and dangerous animals strongly suggests that even humans with grapefruit-sized brains possessed social structure and presumably a relatively sophisticated culture.

Furthermore, that they were able to survive for tens of thousands of years on a tiny island amongst formidable companions such as large monitor lizards that approached or exceeded the size of modern Komodo Dragons, and a dwarf species of an elephant called *Stegodon,* indicate that this miniature human was fully able to successfully coexist in the face of great dangers and great opportunities. In fact, cut and charred *Stegodon* bones found in the cave deposits suggest that this bantam-sized elephant may also have been a food source for the littlest Floresians.

Geological evidence suggests that *H. floresiensis* lived from roughly 95,000 years ago to a mere 13,000 years ago. No doubt 130 centuries prior seems extreme, but this places *H. floresiensis* well within the range of modern humans. If, as archaeological evidence suggests, the East Indies and other islands of Southeast Asia were colonized by humans like us about 18,000-30,000 years ago, then the two species probably coexisted for thousands of years. If so, then once again we discover that oral histories of natives are sometimes based on hard fact.

A Paper Spate

Announcement of the discovery of the hobbits of Flores produced a flurry of papers reporting the discovery, meaning, and the significance of the hobbits. The astonishing nature of the discovery also produced an outpouring of articles in newspapers and magazines aimed specifically at the general public. Although the discovery was much heralded in the countries of the Pacific Rim, virtually every newspaper (*The New York Times, LA Times, Washington Post*, for example) ran one or even a series of articles about the newest humans. The discovery also rated a spot in *Wikipedia: The Free Encyclopedia*, which can be accessed online via *Homo floresiensis* or hobbits as search titles. However, using "hobbits" as a search title will produce many websites that deal with J.R.R. Tolkien's hobbits rather than the topic of our interest.

For the more scientifically inclined general public, *Scientific America* started off with an article entitled "The Littlest Human," which appeared in February 2005. *National Geographic Magazine* ran an exceptionally well-illustrated article that featured illustrations of hobbits and their island habitats. Cryptozoologists also were quick to take an interest in the hobbit story with Loren Coleman taking the lead in announcing its importance, plus the potential of this discovery for research in the often maligned field of cryptozoology. Almost everyone, it seems, had fun with the latest scientific discovery, presenting the news in remarkably appealing fashion.

Unfortunately, not everyone had fun with the diagnosis of hobbits as long lost members of the human clan. For some, the fossils and the media attention that followed aroused a furor rarely seen in scientific circles. Teku Jacob of the Gadjah Madia University in Yogyakara, Indonesia, quickly ignited a controversy by suggesting that the hobbit fossil finds actually represented a group of microcephalic pygmies rather than a new species of Homo. Jacob bolstered his arguments by noting that the fossil bones were found near an area inhabited by modern pygmies. Jacob's skepticism was echoed by three other scientists: Alan Thorne of Australian National University, Robert Eckhardt of Pennsylvania State University, and Maciej Henneberg of the University of Adelaide, also in Australia. Jacob was able to arrange for the transfer of hobbit fossils to his lab in Yogyakara. After several months of examination, Jacob returned the bones to the Center for Archaeology in Jakarta. Based on his analysis of the hobbit bones, Jacob and his crew again reiterated that they represented aberrant humans and nothing more.

The return of the fossils to their discoverer, Michael Morwood, sparked yet another controversy. Morwood reported that some of the delicate and irreplaceable bones had been broken and others damaged. Morwood suggested that the molding process performed by Jacob's team was poorly done, breaking a jawbone in half and causing loss of some anatomical detail in a cranium. Jacob countered that the bones were shipped intact and that any damage occurred during the shipment back to Jakarta. On the other hand, Jacob also stated that his team had put some of the bones together---in a word, "reconstructed" some of the remains but insists that this procedure was done so the fossils could be better studied and analyzed. Others have more unkindly suggested that Jacob actually broke the jawbones while trying to make them fit them into the pattern of a modern jawbone. It bears mentioning that reworking fossils to fit one's preconceptions or prejudices is well outside normal scientific endeavor. Overall, it was not a good day for the science of archeology or paleontology.

To settle the controversy as to whether the hobbits represent a new hominid species or are simply diseased or otherwise misshapen members of *Homo sapiens,* Dean Falk and her team at Florida State University in Tallahassee used advanced technology to create a virtual endocast of the hobbit's brain. The Falk team compared the virtual endocast with brain casts of a true human microcephalic, a *H. sapiens*, a human pygmy, a fossil cranium of *Australopithecus africanus, Paranthropus aeithiopicus,* and the cranium of a chimpanzee (*Pan troglodytes*). On the basis of their work, Falk and her team were able to determine that the structure of the hobbit brain differed substantially from that of a human microcephalic, giving further and very substantial weight to the original proposal that the fossils do, in fact, represent a new species.

The Falk team further suggested that the shape of the hobbit, including the smaller teeth, narrow nose, and shape of braincase and thickness of its cranial bones strongly indicated that they were derived from relic populations of *Homo erectus* that colonized this part of southeast Asia many hundreds of thousands of years ago.

This pronouncement also effectively rules out the idea that the hobbits are yet another type of pygmy, which have small bodies but relatively normal sized brains. In fact, the hobbits do not represent an evolutionary/ecological adaptation of an earlier population of *Homo sapiens* on Flores.

How Do Hobbits and Other Little People Become Little?

Reduced stature in humans and other animals is a side issue but are of interest to us in the context of the origin of little people, or perhaps we should say little peoples. From an ecological standpoint, reduction in body size most frequently occurs as a response to limited food resources. Such circumstances favor the survival of smaller individuals of a population simply because they require less food. Over time natural selection will result in a population of smaller sized individuals.

The two habitats in which reduced stature in humans and many other species most often occur are on islands and within densely forested habitats such as the tropical rain forests of the world. The two very different types of habitat share a major characteristic that drives selection towards smaller size in animals and that is lack of food resources.

The case for smaller-sized individuals on islands is scientifically termed endemic insular dwarfing. The reasons for dwarfing are simple and obvious. An island's smaller natural area will naturally result in less productivity; put another way, a one-acre wheat field will produce half as much wheat as a two-acre wheat field. Among populations of island animals, smaller individuals require less food and so are more likely to survive in an island habitat with reduced food resources. Thus, over time, natural selection will result in insular dwarfing that we find in these little humans, as well as many other species of animals that colonize islands.

Stegodon provides an example of how insular dwarfing can occur. *Stegodon* was one of the largest elephants ever to exist. Adult males stood 13 feet high at the shoulder and were 24 feet long from tail to tip of trunk. Their tusks were a magnificent 10 feet in length and so close together that, unlike modern elephants, the trunk could not fit between, but was laid on top. *Stegodon* probably originated in Africa and spread into Asia. *Stegodon* fossils from Flores indicate that this otherwise mammoth of an elephant had shrunk to a mere 1.5 to 2 meters in height during its insular isolation on the island, which may have been for hundreds of thousands of years.

Dwarfish humans are even better known from rainforest habitat of equatorial Africa, Asia, and Melanesia----we call them pygmies. The African pygmies are small, generally averaging about 1.5 meters, or 4 foot 11 inches in height. Both the Semang peoples and Andamanese peoples are even smaller at four and a half feet in height. All of these small peoples inhabit dense rain forests of the world.

Like their insular kin, the pygmies of the world represent a size-scaling adaptation to lack of nutrient resources. At first this seems incongruous, as tropical rain forests rank as the most productive terrestrial habitats on earth. The problem is that almost all of their productivity is in the phyllosphere, or upper layers of vegetation. In contrast, the environment of the forest floor is almost sterile. Even tropical forest soils are infertile as nutrients released from decomposing plant leaf litter are quickly reabsorbed and incorporated in tree tissue or leached away by the incessant tropical rains.

Reduced stature in tropical rain forests is also beneficial for regulating body temperature; the smaller size of pygmies promotes evaporative cooling, thereby providing a thermoregulatory advantage in hot and humid environments of tropical rain forests. This trend towards smaller sized primates in forested habitats extends to our primate cousins as well. The Bonobo (*Pan paniscus*) is the smaller cousin of the chimpanzee (*Pan troglodytes*). It is confined to the Congo rain forest south of the Congo River.

The Cryptozoology Connection

Such clang is heard along the skies when, from incessant showers
Escaping, and from winter's cold, the cranes
Take wing and over ocean speed away
Woe to the land of dwarfs! Prepared, they fly
For slaughter of the small pigmean race.
– *The Iliad*, Book Three, Homer (translated by Cowper)

So pervasive are tales, rumors, and myths of miniature humans that both Bernard Heuvelemans and Willy Ley devote chapters to "little people" in their best selling books. Heuvelemans entitled his chapter "The Little Hairy Men." In it, Heuvelemans concentrates on the *agogwe*, which are rumored to be little furry men of Africa. He first considers whether these little upright creatures represent sightings of pygmies or even bushman because of their size, which was reported as 4-5 feet in height, which is considerably larger than that reported for the hobbits of Flores and more within the range of modern pygmies. Heuvelemans concludes his chapter by boldly advancing the suggestion that some of these *agogwe* sightings may represent relic populations of *Australopithecines*, the distant ancestor of humans that roamed this continent about 2 million years ago. Since, in Heuveleman's words, the thick forests of Africa are "the last refuge of so many relic species might not the *Australopithecus*'s descendents still survive?"

Willey Ley entitled his chapter simply "The Little People." Ley is also concerned about the possible little people-pygmy connection and suspects that many of these sightings are really of African pygmies and Asian pygmies, or negritos as he terms them. Still, like Heuvelemans, Ley catalogs the series of sightings, discusses the possible pygmy connection, then concludes (like Heuvelemans again) that at least some of these miniatures may represent relic populations of *Australopithecus*, the small ape-like human that was the immediate ancestor of *Homo erectus*, which in turn was the immediate ancestor of *Homo sapiens*.

In Africa, at least, the pygmies are no doubt a likely candidate for some, perhaps many, of the chronicled sightings of "little people." Although lost to history for well over a thousand years, not to be rediscovered until the mid 1800's, the pygmies of Africa were apparently well known to the Ancients: Homer alludes to fights between cranes and pygmies in *The Iliad* and such combats were a classical motif on period vases and other ancient Greek and Roman pottery. The Greek historian and compiler of all facts, Aristotle, devotes a passage of his *Natural History* to pygmy stories, later to be copied by Pliny and still later by Albertus Magnus: "The cranes fly from the Scythian plains to the swamps situated beyond Upper Egypt, whence the Nile comes. These areas are inhabited by pygmies. This is no myth, there actually exists a small tribe, and even their horses are small, their habits are said to be those of Troglodites."

So enamored were the Ancients with these miniature humans that the pharaoh of Ancient Egypt instructed his servants to "come northward immediately bringing the dwarfs from the land of spirits." Pygmies were also in great demand to entertain the crowds that gathered at the Roman coliseum.

Today's pygmies number about 120,000 and still occupy the thickest tropical rain forests of central Western Africa, generally within 5 degrees north or south of the Equator. Here they hunt small mammals and birds with poison-tipped arrows, snare forest birds with nets, and catch serpents in pit traps. Like seemingly all primitive tribes, pygmies are rapidly becoming culturally diluted with their African neighbors, resulting in a physical and cultural mix as they intermarry with members of non-pygmy tribes. Although not actually measured and apparently little discussed, this has probably resulted in a slowly increasing height of the population as a whole – at least if we are to believe accounts of the Ancients, to whom the pygmies were small and spirit-like dwarfs scarcely four feet tall.

Beyond the Indian Mount, or Faerie Elves,
Whose midnight Revels, by a Forest side.
Or Fountain some belated Peasant sees,
Or dreams he sees.
—John Milton, *Paradise Lost*

Native Tales, Little People and Collective Memories

So why should cryptozoologists care about the announcement of yet another fossil find? Because, this fossil bears on the perennial question that we addressed in the first paragraph of this article. For the first time, we now have scientific proof that "little people" by whatever names they had been called by native peoples of the world actually existed – at least in the past. Furthermore, their existence coincided well within the range of modern humans.

There are two distinct explanations for the persistent reports of "little people" that have been rumored or reported throughout modern human history. One possibility is that relic populations still exist, and this possibility provides fertile fuel for cryptozoology. Another explanation is that these rumors and reports really represent memories, myths, legends, folklore, and traditions of little people of past times that have persisted down to the present day.

People have long memories, especially when these memories are incorporated into native myth, folklore, and traditions. The Trojan War is a familiar example, stemming from Homer's account, which was apparently written in around 800-700 BC; that is, several hundred years after the actual war took place around 1250 BC. An even better example is the epic story of the Great Flood, preserved in the Biblical Story of Noah, in the folk tales of Australian aborigines, and in the Babylonian account of Gilgamesh; the latter still to be read from cuneiform tablets recovered from that lost city of Biblical note.

Many scholars suggest that these tales of a Great Flood faithfully preserve the memory of the great floods resulting from the enormous rise in sea level following the melting of the glaciers at the end of the last Ice Age, an event which took place 8,000-10,000 years prior geologically but only a few thousand years before the accounts were converted into a permanent written record.

If these epic tales embedded in human folklore are based on true events, then the case can be made that stories of "little peoples" may also be founded on hard facts.

Granting Scientific Kudos to Cryptozoology?

"There are races of dwarf trees, and why should there not be races of dwarf men?" questioned French explorer Paul B. DuChaillu over a hundred years ago. DuChaillu's sentiments were echoed by Sutikan and his associates who concluded their recent (2004) paper announcing the discovery of *Homo floresiensis* by stating "We anticipate further discoveries of highly endemic, (small) hominin species in locations similarly affected by long-term genetic isolation..."

In a similar vein, Henry Gee, the editor of the prestigious British science journal *Nature* noted that "The discovery that *Homo floresiensis* survived until so very recently in geological terms, makes it more likely that stories of other mythical, human-like creatures such as the Yetis are founded on grains of truth – now cryptozoology, the study of such fabulous creatures, can come in from out of the cold."

We join with Gee, DuChaillu, Sutikan, Ley, and Heuvelmans in anticipating further discoveries, especially since insular dwarfism and sylvidwarfism both represent ecological responses to diminished resources that still continue to this day in certain human populations. Or, to paraphrase previous workers and writers, it is possible that relic populations of *Homo erectus* and possibly even *Australopithecus* or their fossil remains or modern kin are still out there, awaiting or avoiding discovery---maybe even elves, gnomes, and Yeti?

BIBLIOGRAPHY/REFERENCES

Bailey, R. C., and T. Headland. 1991. "The tropical rain forest. Is it a productive habitat for human foragers?" *Human Ecology* 19: 261-285.

Balter, Michael. 2004. "Skeptic to take possession of Flores Hominid bones." *Science* 306: 1450.

Balter, Michael. 2005. "Small but smart? Flores Hominid shows signs of advanced brain." *Science* 307: 1386-1388.

Baltern, Michael. 2005. "'Hobbit' bones go home to Jakarta." *Science* 307: 1386.

Bohannan, Paul, and Philip Curtin. 1995. *Africa and the Africans.* 4th Edition. Waveland Press. Prospect Heights, Illinois. 301 pages.

Brown, P., T. Sutikna, M. J. Morwood, R. P. Soejono, Jatmiko, E. Wayhu Saptomo, and Rokus Awe Due. "A new small-bodied hominin from the Late Pleistocene of   Flores, Indonesia." *Nature* 431: 1055-1061.

Cavalli-Sforza, L.L. (ed). 1986. *African Pygmies.* Academic Press.

Oxford and New York.

Coleman, Loren. 2004. "The top cryptozoology stories of 2004." *The Cryptozoologist* http://lorencoleman.com.

Culotta, Elizabeth. 2005. "Battle erupts over the 'Hobbit'" bones. *Science* 307: 1179.

DuChaillu, Paul B. 1870. "Equatorial Africa, with an account of a race of pigmies." *Journal American Geographical and Statistical Society* 2: 99-112.

Falk, Dean, C. Hildebolt, K. Smith, M. J. Morwood, T. Sutikna, P. Brown, J. Atmiko, E. W. Saptomo, B. Frunsden, and F. Prior. 2005. "The brain of LB1, *Homo floresiensis*." *Science* 8 April 2005; 308: 242-245.

Galdikas, Birute, M. F., Nancy Erickson Briggs, Lori K. Sheeran, Gary L. Shapiro, and Jane Goodall. *All Apes Great and Small: Volume One: African Apes.* KluwerAcademic/Plenum Publishers. New York, New York. 298 pages.

Gee, Henry. 2004. "Flores, God, and Cryptozoology." *Nature.* 27 October 2004.

Gibbs, James L. Jr. Editor. 1965. *The Peoples of Africa.* Holt, Rinehart, and Winston, Inc. New York and San Francisco, 594 pages.

Heuvelmans, Bernard. 1955. *On the Track of Unknown Animals.* Rupert Hart-Davis. London, England, 306 pages.

Ley, Willy. *Exotic Zoology.* Viking Press. Capricorn Books. New York, New York, 468 pages.

Lomolino, M. V. 1985. "Body size of mammals on islands; the island rule reexamined." *American Naturalist* 125: 310-316.

Morwood, Mike. J., R. P. Soejono, R. G. Roberts, T. Sutikna, C. S. M. Turney, K. E. Westaway, W. J. Rink, J-xZhao, G. D. van den Bergy, Rokus Awe Due, D. R. Hobbs, M. W. Moore, M.I. Bird and L. K. Fifield. 2004. "Archaeology and age of a new hominin from Flores in Eastern Indonesia." *Nature* 431: 1087-1091.

Morwood, Mike J., Thomas Tutikna, and Richard Roberts. 2005. "Lost world of the little people." *National Geographic* 4-14, April 2005.

Smith, D. G., and G. A. Mangiacopra. "The literature of the little people." *North American Biofortean Review* 7: 19-22.

Wong, Kate. 2005. "The littlest human." *Scientific American* 291: 56-65.

ACKNOWLEDGMENTS

Although all poetic segments are original, we obtained some of them directly from Bernard Heuvelmans "*On the Track of Unknown Animals.*" The classical segments just fit into the article correctly, so we, as Heuvelmans did before us, have incorporated them at specific points in our narrative.

DWIGHT SMITH teaches biology at Southern Connecticut State University in New Haven, Connecticut. He is very interested in investigating and evaluating the biology and ecology of reputed and reported wildlife of all forms.

GARY MANGIACOPRA lives in Milford, Connecticut. He has devoted thousands of research hours to cryptozoology topics.

MICROBE SAILORS OF THE STARLIGHT
IN THE SCIENCE OF EXTRATERRESTRIAL LIFE, THE LEGACY OF THE BLACKLIST REMAINS
By Roger A. Hart

Nearly half a century ago, three reputable scientists reported anomalous evidence of extraterrestrial life in meteorites, in interstellar space, and on Mars. The scientific community discredited them. Careers were ruined, funding cut-off, and, in one case, the Nobel Prize denied. Yet, recent discoveries indicate these scientists were right. Life on Earth evolved from microbes that had been disseminated throughout the galaxy by starlight. The question remains--why wasn't the public aware of the work of these scientists?

Diamonds from the Sky

Bartholomew Nagy, an organic chemist at Bronx's Fordham University, was the first to study cosmic microbes. In the late 1950s he examined microscopic images of carbonaceous chondrites, unusual meteorites made up of a strange mixture of substances.

Nagy's early study focused on a large carbonaceous chondrite that exploded in a luminous fireball near the French town of Orgueil on May 14, 1864. About 20 head-sized stones crashed to earth in an area of several square kilometers. The carbon-rich specimens, soft enough to be cut with a knife, could be sharpened and used like a pencil.

Recent evidence indicates that the Orguiel meteorite broke off from a comet that had gleaned minerals, gases, and ices from a primordial cloud of dust and gas. The matrix of Orgueil consists of carbon-rich minerals such as diamonds and silica carbide that had been precipitated by a shock wave during the explosion of a star. Gravity pulled the gas and dust from the explosion together in a cloud, the presolar nebula. Further condensation produced the sun, planets, and a hollow sphere of comets surrounding the solar system. Some of the comets adopted elliptical orbits that periodically brought them to the inner solar system. Upon approaching the sun, fragments broke off to form tails, leaving debris in the path of the Earth. Upon encounter, some fragments ignited in fireballs as they plunged through Earth's atmosphere bringing a precious cargo of organic matter and water to the surface.

These facts were unknown to scientists in the early 1950s. By happy accident, Bartholomew Nagy had chosen a meteorite that, we now know, contains carbon from an extinct star system. But the choice turned out to be like a curse.

In 1961, Nagy and microbiologist George Claus described filamentary formations, similar to microscopic terrestrial algae, preserved in the Orgueil meteorite. After eliminating known terrestrial contaminants and discussing their results with colleagues, Nagy and Claus wrote in the journal *Nature*, "We are of the opinion that the organized elements are microfossils apparently indigenous to the meteorite parent body." The curse kicked in right away.

Skeptics viciously attacked Nagy and argued that the "organized elements" were nothing more than contamination – museum dust and pollen. Before Nagy could answer his critics, they uncovered a hoax that forever tipped the balance of the argument against him.

The Orgueil meteorite had first arrived on the scientific scene about the time when Louis Pasteur was arguing against spontaneous generation of life from spiritual sources; microscopic spores or seeds preceded all life according to Pasteur. He examined the Orgueil meteorite and pronounced it devoid of life. Evidently some proponents of spontaneous generation decided to perpetrate a hoax on Pasteur. Using gum and coal fragments, they glued a plant stem and seed capsules to fragments of the Orgueil meteorite before it was sealed in a glass jar in Montauban, France. They imagined Pasteur would be surprised to find a plant had spontaneously generated from a lifeless meteorite.

When researchers, hoping to corroborate Nagy's results, requested specimens of the Orgueil meteorite from Montauban, they discovered the plant fragment. Plagued by bad luck, Nagy was forever linked to the hoax perpetrated almost a century before without his involvement or knowledge. Nagy attempted to defend his position by pointing out that his "organized elements" were fossilized and therefore could not be of terrestrial origin. But his voice was lost in the clamor that broke out.

"Case closed," said the critics. The vocal majority had overruled.

Nagy's few supporters were similarly silenced. Harold Urey, one of the world's leading cosmic chemists, wrote in *Science* in 1966 that had the "organized elements" been found in sedimentary rock on earth, there would have been no question that they were biological in origin. Also in 1966, British scientists W.C. Tan and Sam L. VanLandingham reported a new study of the suspected fossils in Orgueil and published pictures of them in the *Journal of the Royal Astronomical Society.*

In 1975, Nagy, then at the University of Arizona in Tucson, published his book, *Carbonaceous Meteorites*, describing expanded studies of carbonaceous meteorites from Ivuna, Africa and Revelstoke, Canada in addition to the one from Orgueil. What appear to be fossil remains of microbes including cellular structures were illustrated in the book and Nagy maintained that they were from extraterrestrial sources.

Nagy's critics identified clear evidence of pollen from terrestrial plants among his illustrations. In the world of science, sadly, even one error can discredit an otherwise sound study. Nagy's few supporters did little to avert the tide of negativity gathering around him. Prominent pollen expert Elso Barghoorn concluded that the "organized elements" indigenous to the meteorites were not pollen and were of extraterrestrial origin. Later studies of similar "organized elements" were accepted as evidence of extraterrestrial life. But because there was evidence that some of Nagy's "organized elements" were questionable, the entire study was disregarded. We were denied the results of his discovery for decades. For his part, Nagy discreetly retreated.

The debate was reopened with studies of a carbonaceous chondrite that fell near the small town of Murchison, Victoria, Australia on September 28, 1969. The parent object disintegrated in the air and scattered fragments over an area of five square miles of pastures. The fall was witnessed and local residents immediately collected specimens.

The initial work on amino acids in the Murchison samples, done in the laboratories of NASA Ames research center, led to convincing evidence of amino acids of extraterrestrial origin. More than fifty of the amino acids found in Murchison are not present on Earth and have extraterrestrial isotopic signatures.

In 1979, German paleontologist Hans Dietrich Pflug found fossilized cells and virus particles in the Murchison meteorite, equivalent to those discovered in the Orgueil meteorite by Nagy. Pflug considered the arguments for and against Earthly contamination as the source for the fossils and became convinced that they came from space.

Astronomer Fred Hoyle defended Pflug's discovery. "When Pflug found carbonized samples of that bacteria–true clusters of them–in the meteorite, the question that until then was controversial started leaning to the side of Nagy and Claus, so vehemently silenced twenty years before. Finally, clear proof of the existence of extraterrestrial life could be observed."

Nagy passed away in 1995. To the end, he insisted that the microfossils that he found were extraterrestrial life forms. "Perhaps it is well not to draw conclusions," he wrote, "but it appears most likely that the carbonaceous compounds and small carbonaceous objects found in these meteorites would be confidently assumed to be of biological origin if found on earth."

There is no evidence that all of his "organized elements" were contamination. Recent studies have exonerated Nagy, but his work remains unacknowledged after 45 years.

Why wasn't Nagy's work accepted? The rejection of his data based on a few errors was too sweeping to be based on science alone. Was politics involved in some way? Was there a need to protect secret government work? Were NASA scientists trying to cover up their own errors or keep the rights to the discovery of extraterrestrial life for themselves?

The Secret Life of Stardust

While Bartholomew Nagy and his colleagues gathered the evidence from meteorites found on Earth, amazing insights came from space itself.

Sir Fred Hoyle, one of the most distinguished scientists of the 20th century, was born in Yorkshire, the son of a wool merchant. By the age of ten he could navigate by the stars. He moved on to Cambridge, where he studied mathematics. During World War ll, the British Admiralty engaged him in technical projects.

Hoyle returned to Cambridge after the war as university lecturer in mathematics, and soon focused on problems of accretion of dust and gas around astronomical bodies. In 1958, he was appointed the Plumian professor of astronomy and became the first director of the Cambridge Institute of Theoretical Astronomy in 1967. He served on the council of the Royal Society as vice president from 1969 to 1971, was knighted in 1972 and awarded the royal medal of the Royal Society in 1974. On that occasion, the president of the Royal Society said that Hoyle was one of the most original minds in astronomy.

His work on the theory of nucleogenesis, the build-up of the elements in stars, was an outstanding scientific landmark of the 1950s. In the development of this theory Hoyle collaborated on a paper with W.A. Fowler of the California Institute of Technology in Pasadena, and with Geoffrey and Margaret Burbidge. The paper showed that, starting with hydrogen, nuclear fusion could produce the elements in the hot interiors of stars. The theory explained the relative abundances of the elements, provided an explanation of the direction of stellar evolution, and gave an objective basis for calculation of the internal constitution of stars.

The paper, published in *Reviews of Modern Physics* in 1957, has been described as monumental, and the theory has had a cardinal influence on astrophysics. Although there were four authors, it is widely known that the Burbidges contributed the data from their stellar observations and that the core and essence of the paper was the work of Fowler and Hoyle.

Hoyle turned his attention to the space between the stars. Gas and dust left over from exploded stars is ubiquitous and, in places, concentrated in immense clouds containing an amazing array of chemical compounds. Hoyle joined with Chandra Wickramasinghe in a study of the chemical composition of the dust between the stars. Every molecule has a unique fingerprint, a kind of bar code of identification that is uniform throughout the universe. In the 1960s Hoyle and Chandra Wickramasinghe discovered that the bar code of graphite, a mineral made of carbon, matched that of interstellar dust.

Over time Hoyle and Wickramasinghe realized that some other carbon-rich molecule was present in addition to graphite. They searched through the records of thousands of compounds and in 1974 finally hit on sugar or some polysaccharide with similar properties. To them this seemed like a straightforward transition from inorganic to organic carbon compounds. Unexpectedly, their conclusion reverberated badly with the scientific community.

Since then, other astronomers have identified over fifty organic molecules in interstellar dust clouds. Meanwhile, Hoyle and Wickramasinghe continued to push the envelope of credibility.

The refractive index of some components of interstellar dust is unusually low. For years Hoyle and Wickramasinghe worked to identify a model that would match the stardust's barcode for the broadest range of spectral frequencies and physical properties. When a model with freeze-dried bacteria produced a near-perfect match in 1979, they bravely published it. That work has been harshly criticized, but competing nonbiological models do not match the data nearly as well. The criticism was not against their interpretation of the data but fell along the line of "That's crazy, where did all the bacteria come from?"

Hoyle and Wickramasinghe replied that they were merely reporting an observation, not proposing a theory of the origin of life. According to the scientific method, observation precedes explanation. In this case the critics were asking for an explanation before they would accept the observation.

To answer their critics, Hoyle and Wickramasinghe studied the origin and evolution of life. They noticed that dust particles in the tails of comets, most recently that of Hale-Bopp, have the same barcode of spectral and physical properties as those of the interstellar dust. They proposed that microbes traveled in comets and pointed out that if a comet with even one viable microbe landed on a celestial body with water, food, and suitable temperature, life would have rapidly multiplied. Over 100 billion nebulae have condensed in our galaxy. Any one of them may have nurtured and multiplied microbial life on moons, asteroids, or planets. Impacts with other celestial bodies may have thrown vast numbers of microbes into space ready to inoculate and multiply in a new nebula. As a proponent of the steady state universe, Fred Hoyle believed this universe or some similar universe has always existed. Eternity is plenty of time for life to propagate throughout the cosmos.

Astronomers concur that comets are rich in a tar-like substance and could have delivered much of Earth's water, atmospheric gases, and the carbon compounds from which life molecules are made. The idea of bacteria in comets is still hotly debated.

The subject of extraterrestrial life was still controversial in 1983 when W. G. Fowler was awarded the Nobel Prize for physics. Why Fowler's coauthor, Hoyle, was not included in this award remains a mystery hidden in the confidential documents of the Royal Swedish Academy. The editor of the scientific journal *Nature* suggested that the academy did not wish to be associated with any endorsement of Hoyle's belief that life must be a frequent occurrence in the universe. In itself, this idea would not necessarily be rejected as absurd by the scientific community, but Hoyle had publicized a further argument that epidemics of disease were associated with the passage of the Earth through certain meteor streams, the particles of which conveyed pathogens to Earth.

Fowler himself in an autobiographical sketch affirmed Hoyle's immense contribution: "The grand concept of nucleosynthesis in stars was first definitely established by Hoyle in 1946."

Hoyle and Wickramasinghe diligently continued to gather a logical chain of evidence leading from interstellar space, to comets, to the surface of planets. They maintain that strong evidence for life in space is ignored because it is culturally unacceptable. The critics challenged: If microbes arrived on Earth from outer space, why aren't they present in Earth's upper atmosphere, on other planets, and on the moon? Hoyle and Wickramasinghe responded, "They *are.*"

Earth's upper atmosphere was sampled by balloon in the 1960s. In a series of balloon flights between 1962 and 1965, NASA scientists found bacteria at heights up to 90,000 feet. In 1963, scientists from the Jet Propulsion Laboratory found the density of bacteria increased upward to 130,000 feet. NASA denounced the result as spurious, and funding for the project was cut off. Based on the published balloon results, Hoyle and Wickramasinghe calculated that up to a billion billion viable bacteria might reach the surface of Earth from space every year. Of these, each of us may breathe in about a thousand space-incident bacteria and consume up to another ten thousand in drinking water.

Hoyle and Wickramasinghe suggested patterns of some infectious disease indicate they were introduced by microbes entering Earth's atmosphere from space. In order to pass through Earth's atmosphere without burning up, meteorites must be less than a tenth of a centimeter in diameter. Many smaller microbes, unprotected by meteorite hosts, can survive the trip into the upper atmosphere when the X-ray outbursts from the sun are at a minimum. The microbes would pass through the upper atmosphere at a leisurely pace. Once in the lower atmosphere currents of air and electricity would distribute them in distinct patterns.

Hoyle and Wickramasinghe suggested that diseases that are seasonal, appear out of nowhere, or trace back to more than one point of origin are from space. These include a remarkably localized disease that struck the city of Athens in 430 BC. A major outbreak of bubonic plague, thought to be carried by black rats, occurred in 540-590 AD and killed up to a hundred million victims in the Near East, North Africa, and southern Europe. For the next 800 years the world was spared from the ravages of plague. Then it broke out in the form of the "Black Death" in 1347 in the vicinity of Greece. In a year it had crossed the English Channel. Over the next three centuries, countless millions died including the final episodes that occurred in London in 1664. Strangely, the next 230 years were plague-free. Next, bubonic plague broke out in China and India between 1896 and 1917, killing some 13 million people. Hoyle and Wickramasinghe asked: How is it possible for a disease to be absent from the earth only to reappear centuries later unless pathogenic bacteria were periodically injected from space?

What about the moon? Can bacteria survive without an atmosphere to cushion their impact on the surface? On September 24, 1970, the Soviet Union's Luna 16 spacecraft returned from the moon's Sea of Fertility with 101 grams of lunar soil in a hermetically sealed container. In February 1972, Luna 20 used a drill with a ten-inch, hollow-core bit to collect another soil sample that was also hermetically sealed on the moon. Back in the USSR, the sealed containers from the Luna missions were delivered to the laboratory and the contents immediately photographed under a microscope. Even after hundreds of these pictures were published in an atlas in 1979, the biological nature of some of the particles was not acknowledged. But in 1999 two biologists at the Russian Academy of Sciences, Stanislav I. Zhmur and Lyudmila M. Gerasimenko, discovered that a few of the photographs depicted fossils that resembled the organized elements Bartholomew Nagy had found in carbonaceous chondrites. Perhaps bacteria had arrived on the lunar surface inside a meteorite that had broken open upon impact.

Hoyle and Wickramasinghe also studied the scientific barcode of dust on Mars and, again, it matched the spectrum of freeze-dried bacteria. In 1977, they announced that Martian dust storms uncovered bacteria living below the surface.

Fred Hoyle died on August 20, 2001, staunchly maintaining to the end that microbes populate space, permeate the solar system, rain down on Earth via comets, periodically induce pandemics, and bring new genetic material to life on Earth. Recent evidence suggests Fred Hoyle was right. But his work has not been acknowledged. Were public health authorities concerned that popularization of his results would invoke panic in the public? Was that why he was denied the Noble Prize while his colleague, Fowler, granted one? Do billions of bacteria from space rain down on Earth, the Moon, and Mars everyday?

Publicly, NASA staunchly denied that there was any evidence for extraterrestrial life for three decades. Privately, NASA implemented a plan to protect us from accidental infestation by extraterrestrial life. It established the Office of Planetary Protection.

The Office of Planetary Protection

Nobel Prize winner, Harold Urey, while publicly attacking the results of Bart Nagy, concluded that the possibility remained open that Nagy's organized elements were microbes. Erroneously thinking that the Orgueil meteorite was from the moon, Urey urged that Apollo 11 astronauts returning from the moon in 1969 should be held in quarantine for up to a month.

A protocol for protecting earth from contamination was established by NASA. The protocol mandated that the Apollo 11 command module be retrieved from the Pacific Ocean *unopened* and conveyed to the aircraft carrier U.S.S. Hornet, where the astronauts would walk through an enclosed tunnel to a decontamination chamber.

On July 24, 1969, the Apollo 11 command module splashed down 13 nautical miles from the Hornet in the Pacific Ocean southwest of Hawaii. The travel time required for the Hornet to reach the command module was longer than planned. Fearful for the fate of the astronauts and, with an impatient Richard Nixon waiting to greet them in front of the world television audience, helicopters were dispatched. A Navy diver and a rubber life raft were dropped, the door of the module was *opened*, and biological contamination suits handed to the astronauts inside. The door of the command module was closed for eight minutes while Neil Armstrong, Buss Aldrin, and Michael Collins suited up. They then climbed into the rubber life raft and were airlifted to the carrier by helicopter, where they walked across the open deck to the decontamination container to grin out through a window at a triumphant president Nixon. This was the image of the splashdown engraved in the public mind.

Was Earth contaminated with bacteria from the moon during the opening of the hatch door? Absolutely not, replied NASA, "Because there is no life on the moon."

Was NASA trying to cover up of the failure of the agency to follow protocol of planetary protection? If there was no chance of contamination, why was the door to the command module resealed while the astronauts suited up? Why were the astronauts confined to a quarantine chamber on the Hornet? Why were they held in quarantine for three month in Houston? The exposure of the inside of the Command Module, even for a fraction of a second, could have exposed Earth's atmosphere and oceans to microbes from the moon. The contamination suits could have been infected and microbes released in the life raft, inside the helicopter, and on the deck of the Hornet. But can microbes survive the vacuum on the surface of the moon?

On November 14, 1969, Astronauts from Apollo 12 retrieved a camera from the unmanned Surveyor 3 spacecraft that had landed on the moon on April 17, 1967. Scientists were surprised to find viable *Streptococcus mitis* bacteria on the lens. NASA denied the bacteria were extraterrestrial. NASA *did* acknowledge that bacteria are capable of surviving the vacuum and radiation of space.

"I always thought the most significant thing we found on the whole goddamn Moon was that little bacteria who came back and lived and nobody ever said shit about it," said Apollo 12 astronaut Pete Conrad.

"Contamination from Earth," chanted NASA, a mantra often repeated.

Was bacteria brought back in soil samples by the Russian Luna spacecraft? Were the bacteria from Earth? The soil was hermetically *sealed* in containers on the moon.

The mystery deepened when life on Mars was discovered–and quickly denied.

Life on Mars?

Gilbert V. Levin, after earning engineering degrees from Johns Hopkins University, invented a sensitive apparatus for detecting microbial activity. While working for the Maryland state health department, he added radioactive carbon as a means to "label" nutrient solutions used to test for bacteria in municipal water systems. The radioactive method is so sensitive that as few as ten bacterial cells can be detected in about half an hour. Growth is not needed. The method is now used in hospitals and clinics worldwide to detect human blood infection quickly.

The excellent success in rapidly detecting the broadest possible array of microorganisms in soils from around the world and also in laboratory cultures, together with its small and efficient instrumentation, won a spot for Levin's Labeled Release, LR, experiment on the Viking mission to Mars.

"Tests by Viking Hint of Life on Mars" read the headline of *The New York Times* on Aug. 8, 1976. However, when experiments performed on Martian soil produced ambiguous results, an argument broke out among the scientists. NASA officially announced that there is no life on Mars. The announcement diverted attention from the positive result of Levin's experiment.

In the label release experiment, Gilbert Levin and Patricia Straat dropped radiocarbon-tagged amino acid broth on Martian soil retrieved by a sampling arm. They detected radiocarbon tagged gas in their instrument. This meant that the radiocarbon tagged amino acids were consumed and converted into carbon dioxide or methane by heterotrophic bacteria.

Their experiment tested the soil of Mars nine times at two different landing sites under different temperature regimes and environmental conditions. All the data point to microbes metabolizing a nutrient solution and giving off an indicative radioactive gas.

Critics immediately claimed the results were too extreme, that the release of radioactive gas must be the result of an unknown inorganic reaction.

Levin and Straat had an immediate response to the criticism. Heat dampens a biological reaction by killing the microbes. Levin and Straat heated the soil to 160°C and the reaction stopped. At a press conference, Levin reported: "The response we are getting is consistent with the kinds of response we are used to getting in terrestrial soils."

There was strong opposition to any biological conclusion, based primarily on the failure of Viking to detect organic molecules in the soil. Levin and Straat demonstrated that their own experiment was several orders of magnitude more sensitive than the instrument designed to detect organic matter.

Rather than admit Levin and Straat were right, NASA supported the idea that a hitherto unknown hypothetical oxidant must be present in the Martian soil. Many other theories were put forth. These were all capped with the insistence that there could be no liquid water on the surface of Mars, hence no life. The evidence showed that the surface of Mars was too cold for life. Could life survive in such an environment? Levin and Straat reproduced their results on soil in the cold dry valleys of Antarctica.

Levin followed and refuted all the arguments, as, for example, in a 1986 paper to the National Academy of Science, which concluded with the statement that it was then as probable as not that the labeled release experiment had detected life. However, this conclusion was greeted with derision.

Microbes on Mars must live below the surface, shielded from radiation. Recent calculations show, because internal heat increases with depth, that liquid water may be present below the surface. Bacteria on earth can live at great depths without sunlight or oxygen, in some cases burrowing into solid volcanic rock. Stream channels and shorelines on Mars are evidence that the water has periodically erupted to the surface. Could erupting water have brought bacteria to the surface where they hibernated until the warm broth of Gilbert and Levin stirred them back to life? Could dust storms have excavated bacteria colonies below the surface? Could Viking have sampled cosmic bacteria that fell from space to the surface of Mars?

Perhaps new missions will bring back evidence for life on Mars and Levin and Straat will receive the credit they deserve. In the meantime, dazzling discoveries in molecular biology and the microbiology of bacteria provide strong evidence for the colonization of Earth by cosmic microbes.

The Cosmic Heritage of Life on Earth

The discovery of the origin of life is generally regarded as the ultimate quest of science. Did life originate only on Earth? Did it evolve through the process of natural selection? According to Darwinian evolution, *accidental* damage to DNA produces a variety of mutations, some of which are selected to further the development of the species.

If life evolved solely on Earth through evolution, it is a supreme accident. If evidence is found that life originated more than once, then unknown laws of nature may be rigged in favor of life. If so, life may exist in countless localities throughout the cosmos.

In the 1950's, Harold Urey and Stanley Miller showed that

simple amino acids could spontaneously develop from a "primordial soup" similar to Earth's early oceans. That experiment is still quoted as decisively showing that life on Earth evolved from simple elements.

Since the Urey-Miller experiment, molecular biologists have discovered hundreds of thousands of complex biochemicals. Simplest life is dependent on a complex system of more than two thousand enzymes. Enzymes are large proteins composed of long chains of twenty amino acids arranged in specific sequences that could not have been produced by random trial even if the whole universe consisted of primordial soup. The odds against shuffling amino acids into the right sequence to form a protein molecule by accident are enormous.

Fred Hoyle likened the odds against the spontaneous assembly of life from simple elements to those for a whirlwind sweeping through a junkyard and producing a functional Boeing 747. The elaborate system of biochemicals in even the simplest bacteria could not have spontaneously evolved from non-biological elements in the lifetime of the Earth.

Most theorists estimate that meteorites bombarded Earth until 3.9 billion years ago. Because of the intolerable heat, the first life must have appeared after that time. The surplus of the lighter isotope of carbon in sedimentary rocks from West Greenland, South Africa, and Australia, shows that life was present on Earth 3.85 billion years ago.

Life appeared on Earth at the earliest possible time. Furthermore, life had a jump-start. The elaborate chemical evolution that must have preceded the formation of the first cell had already been completed.

Biologists, recognizing that cellular life cannot exist without the essential molecules ATP or RNA, have postulated natural reservoirs of pre-biotic molecules and labeled them "ATP world" and "RNA world." Spontaneously generated deposits have not yet been discovered and these molecules are produced in the laboratory only at great expense under extraordinary circumstances.

Then there is the chicken and the egg problem. The manufacture of RNA requires enzymes. But the manufacture of enzymes requires RNA. Which came first, the RNA or the enzyme?

An additional problem has to do with the fact that organisms make a living by drinking in information. The second law of thermodynamics stipulates that an information-rich system cannot spontaneously evolve from information-poor one. The popular version of the second law of thermodynamics is the expression, "There is no free lunch." Some energy and order are converted to entropy in any natural process making perpetual motion impossible. Information requires order and is converted to disorder in any natural process. Information-rich molecules such as complex enzymes cannot spontaneously evolve from information poor molecules such as amino acids. Scientists have begun a search for pre-biotic information that organized the first coded biochemicals. Some researchers believe inorganic minerals such as clay or pyrites provide the information. Others invoke self-organization in turbulent flow systems. To them, life is the result of here-to-fore undiscovered laws of self-organization. So far the problem has not been solved.

Francis Crick, who received the Nobel Prize for unraveling the double helix structure of DNA, proposed that a space probe planted the first coded biochemicals on Earth early in its history. In the forward to the book *RNA World*, Crick writes, "At present, the gap from the primordial soup to the first RNA system capable of natural selection looks forbiddingly wide."

The preponderance of evidence points to one conclusion: Life did not originate on Earth as the result of random accident. Where did it originate? New discoveries about bacteria show they are adapted to an amazing range of possible origins.

Bacteria are uniquely adapted to the radiation, vacuum, and low temperatures of space. Two bacteria, *micrococcus radiodurans* and *micrococcus radiophilus,* can withstand doses of X-rays up to 600 kilorads, Even *E. Coli* the bacteria that assists in the digestion of our food, could survive the x-ray dosage from several large solar flares. As shown during Apollo 12, *Streptococcus mitis* can survive up to two years in absolute vacuum. Bacteria thrive in freezing water trapped beneath the Antarctic ice sheet. Entire communities of bacteria, fungi, lichen, and algae live between the mineral grains of rocks from the dry valleys of Antarctica. Other bacteria can survive in the laboratory after being frozen several hundred degrees below zero. Microbiologists have revived bacteria frozen for 11,000 years in the intestine of a mastodon, encased for 35 million years in amber from Costa Rica, and preserved in a salt deposit for 150 million years. Scientists have revived bacteria that are 250 million years old, strengthening the case that bacterial spores may be immortal.

Bacteria can shrink, dry up, and hibernate by constructing a hard celled endosperm. They revive in a drop of tepid water, and start doubling in as little as three hours. Given unlimited nutrients, energy, and space they can produce up to a thousand tons of biomass in one day.

The new discoveries about bacteria not only demonstrate their unique adaptations to space, but also show that liquid water and oxygen are not necessary for propagation of life in the universe. With an occasional stopover on a friendly world, bacteria might have populated empty space for billions of years.

The Red Giant Hypothesis

Stellar radiation in the form of visible light as well as gamma rays, x-rays, UV-rays, infrared radiation, and radio waves, is energetic enough to propel small masses, such as freeze-dried bacteria, through space. The hottest stars radiate the most energetic radiation. But can microbes escape the gravity field of a star and survive re-entry and impact on a new planet?

Astronomers Jeff Secker from Washington State University and Paul Wesson and James Lepock from the University of Waterloo, Ontario may have come up with answers to these questions. They propose that microbes are propelled through space by radiation from red giants that, being relatively cool, have minimal amounts of lethal high-energy radiation. Red giants are part of the normal cycle of stars, preceding nova and supernova explosions.

Over their lifetime, stars eject matter into space as part of the stellar winds. Small stars like our sun eject light elements such as hydrogen and helium; massive stars eject heavier elements like carbon, oxygen, and nitrogen. One class of red giants, the carbon stars, eject enough carbon to coat microbes.

Stars expand and contract, fueled by the fusion of elements in their core. In the final stage of their life cycle they expand into red giants. Our sun, already about four billion years old will expand as a red giant sometime in the next four billion years and eventually engulf earth in its fiery corona.

Astronomers have detected over 60 extra-solar planets orbiting distant stars. It is likely that many stars have planets, moons, and comets orbiting around them, some of them similar to those in our solar system.

According to the hypothesis, as a red giant expands toward a planet, before destroying it, water and organic matter are vaporized. Boiling atmospheres, evaporating oceans, meteorite impacts, and volcanic eruptions combine to produce towering clouds of steam and ash. The cloud storms launch cool fine dust and organic debris alive with microbes into space. After encasing them in protective pods of carbon, the stellar wind carries the microbes to outer space, where they shift to the currents of stellar radiation. Traveling at speeds up to 50 kilometers per second, the interstellar stowaways can travel to any of the closest 50 stars in about a million years.

Astronomers estimate 200 million red giants have exploded since the birth of our galaxy over 10 billion years ago. About 20 million of these may have scorched planets, moons, or comets. About 2 million red giants, one out of a hundred, may have incinerated planets that harbored simple microbial life.

A new convoy of microbes could launch into the starlight on the average, every 5,000 years. Eventually some of the microbes condense in a cloud around a neophyte planetary system, ultimately hitching rides to the inner planets and moons on comets.

Thousands of house-sized "dark" comets and over 400 billion smaller meteors and dust fragments enter Earth's atmosphere every day, about a pound a second, up to 35,000 tons per year. The rain of cosmic debris increases dramatically every 26 million years, causing mass extinctions and pulses of evolution. About one percent of the dust is from stars beyond our solar system, the rest is left over from comets or the occasional asteroid. Most of the debris disperses in the upper atmosphere; some of it reaches the Earth's surface. Small dust grains, some of them apparently bearing extraterrestrial microbes, impact softly without heating up and accumulate in layers beneath the oceans.

Microbes have made Earth habitable for other forms of life by regulating the output of greenhouse gas. Only those microbes that evolved on a planet with suitable temperatures could survive the billions of years required for a star to reach the red giant stage. As the thermal output of parent stars waxed, the microbes produced less greenhouse gas. As the output of a star waned, the microbes blanketed planets with more greenhouse gas. As millions of red giants expanded and incinerated planets, microbes genetically disposed to regulate a planet's temperature survived to be launched into the starlight.

Microbes small enough to sail the starlight carry enough genetic information to rival the works of Shakespeare. Once seeded on a new home they can revive and initiate a new cycle of life that, given enough time, can evolve to the richness of life on Earth.

Sugar-Coating the Results

After denying the possibility of extraterrestrial life for over thirty years, NASA announced a dramatic reversal of policy in 1996. Over the next decade, a series of discoveries confirmed the earlier work of Nagy, Hoyle, and Levin.

Just a few months after Bartholomew Nagy died in 1995, President Clinton announced that NASA had discovered extraterrestrial life in the meteorite, ALH84001, reportedly ejected from Mars and collected in Antarctica. Nagy might have flipped in his grave if he had heard the news. There was nothing essentially new in the Martian meteorite that wasn't present in the Orgueil and Murchison meteorites studied by Nagy decades before. Photographs of the Martian meteorite taken by scanning electron microscope showed extremely small forms—perhaps too small. The images showed organized elements no bigger than the wall of a normal bacteria cell. Also, it turned out that some of the minerals formed at temperatures above 600ºC, too high to support life.

Why make a fuss over questionable life forms in the Martian meteorite 35 years after Nagy first published his observations? The answer appears to be cultural rather than scientific. Society was not ready to accept the idea of extraterrestrial life in 1961. After decades of movies depicting extraterrestrial life, from the cuddly *E.T.* to the fearsome monsters in *Alien*, or the grotesque machines of *War of the Worlds*, the collective psyche hardly stirs at the thought of extinct bacteria from Mars. In *War of the Worlds*, it is microbes that save the humans. Whether or not the evidence for life in the Martian meteorite ALH84001 holds up with time, public exposure to the data has been a watershed in the collective acceptance of extraterrestrial life.

Announcements of new evidence followed in rapid succession.

On July 29, 1997, Richard B. Hoover of NASA's Marshall Space Flight Center announced the discovery of fossilized extraterrestrial bacteria in the Murchison meteorite. Furthermore the surrounding amino acids were clearly extraterrestrial. Subsequently, microfossils were discovered in the Allende carbonaceous chondrite that fell in Pueblito de Allende, Mexico on February 28, 1969.

On July 30, 1997, Gilbert Levin called a press conference and announced that for twenty years he had answered all challenges to his discovery of life on Mars in 1976. According to Levin, "of all the many hypotheses offered over the years to explain the Mars Labeled Release results, the only possibility fitting all the relevant data is that microbial life exists in the top layer of the Martian surface."

One of the main criticisms of his discovery was that no organic carbon had been found in the soil and that there was no water on the surface of Mars. Earthbound spectroscopic studies of Mars have shown there is both methane and ethane in the atmosphere of Mars. Furthermore, there is a distinct band of methane erupting from fissures at Mars' equator. On Earth most of the methane and ethane are produced biologically.

In addition, recent NASA missions have discovered signs of water ice on the surface of Mars. In 2000, Mars Global Surveyor sent back images of gullies recently carved by running water. In May 2002, Mars Odyssey found water in shallow polar soil. With the evidence of water, the odds that Mars once had life and still has life today have gone up significantly.

Will liquid water be discovered on the surface of Mars? Most scientists concur that it occurs below the surface. Heat produced inside Mars by the decay of Uranium and other radioactive elements may be focused in hotspots that periodically cause volcanic eruptions like the ones that occur on Iceland or Yellowstone Park. Invasion of hot magma from below, eruption of volcanic rocks on the surface, and the impact of meteors and spacecraft can melt ice just below the surface. Perhaps dormant bacteria in the surface soil layers on Mars come to life when they periodically find a pool of liquid water to flourish in.

In regards to his critics Levin concludes, "They show a somewhat amateurish, but still strongly biased approach with respect to microbiological technique, the use of appropriate controls, the interpretation of results, and the use of long-dead straw-men arguments in a vain attempt to cover up, rather than to discuss objectively, the results of the Mars Viking LR experiment." Levin thinks NASA is crippled by the fear of finding out that its original conclusion about Viking was wrong.

On January 4, 1999, NASA officially recognized the possibility that life on Earth came from space. Later that year, NASA announced the formation of a task force to establish how scientists will evaluate evidence in the search for extraterrestrial life. The task force will have three primary goals: to evaluate and agree upon known terrestrial biomarkers, to identify the ones from that list that may be applicable to Mars, and to identify biomarkers that have not been used for Earth, but might possibly be used for Mars. NASA is clearly looking ahead to the possibility of discovering life during a Mars sample return mission.

What about Hoyle? Have his results been confirmed? The Stardust Mission, launched toward Comet Wilde 2 in 1997, collected and analyzed stardust in 2000. The results confirmed the 1977 observation of Hoyle and Wickramasinghe that large molecules of sugar exist in stardust. One prediction of their model has been borne out.

"The discovery of cross-linked hetero-aromatic polymers in interstellar dust by instruments aboard the Stardust spacecraft would confirm the validity of the biological grain model that was suggested from spectroscopic studies over 20 years ago. Such structures could represent fragments of cell walls that survive 30km/s impacts onto detector surfaces," Hoyle and Wickramasinghe wrote in the May 1, 2000 issue of *Astrophysics and Space Science.*

The Stardust Mission collected dust from Comet P/Wilde2 in the year 2004 and returned it to Earth in February 2006. The collection medium, a brittle aerogel, is too hard to permit the implantation of light desiccated bacteria. There is the possibility that bacteria entrained in larger fragments will turn up in the millions of microscopic images examined by online volunteers.

Shortly before his death on August 20, 2001, Fred Hoyle lamented that no NASA experiment since Viking of 1976 has been designed specifically to test for extraterrestrial life.

Shortly after Fred Hoyle's death, George Cooper and co-workers at NASA's Ames Research Center, Moffett Field, California reported sugar-like substances in a meteorite. Sugars and the closely related compounds discovered by Cooper, collectively called "polyols," are critical to all known life forms. "This discovery shows that it's highly likely organic synthesis critical to life has gone on throughout the universe," said Kenneth A. Souza, acting director of astrobiology and space research at Ames. "Then, on Earth, since the other critical elements (water and nutrients) were in place, life could blossom."

On August 2, 2004, Nagy's studies of the Orguiel meteorite were dramatically confirmed. Richard Hoover of NASA's Marshall Space Flight Center revealed high-tech images from a freshly fractured specimen of the meteorite that showed forms that closely resemble mats of known terrestrial fossilized cyanobacteria, not just isolated single cells, but whole ecologies that cannot be logically dismissed as either mineral grains or post-arrival microbial contaminants. The images showed lithified microfossils tightly conjugated with the mineral matrix, removing the possibility that they are contaminants.

Recent studies also shed light on the origin of the Orgueil meteorite. The matrix of carbon dust contains a type of xenon gas that is not found in our present solar system. Recent studies of unusual amino acids link the Orgueil specimens to a comet similar to Hale-Bopp. The mother comet of the Orguiel meteorite passed close enough to the sun for ice to melt and hot water to circulate between the original minerals depositing veins of water-rich minerals impregnated with rare elemental nickel. The Orgueil comet with a history of liquid water combined with carbon derived from a now extinct star is the perfect candidate to carry life from interstellar space to the inner planets of our solar system.

Hoover discussed the reasons Bartholomew Nagy's earlier results were contested. Hoover believes the scientific community could not accept the idea that microbes could live in volcanic rocks. Recent discoveries about extremophiles, microbes that carve out a niche under extreme conditions including volcanic rocks, make it easier to accept the most recent results from Orgueil. The physicist, Tom Gold, has compiled evidence showing that more bacteria may be living beneath the surface of the Earth than above. Volcanic rocks recovered from hundreds of meters inside the Earth have tunnels excavated by rock-consuming bacteria. These bacteria, rather than deriving their energy from the sun, derive it from the chemicals in the rocks.

"It really isn't correct to say this question of the organized elements was closed 30 years ago." Hoover argues, "Although some of the Nagy forms were indeed pollen and other contaminants, there were also many other bodies found in these meteorites by Nagy and other researchers of the period that were clearly not pollen. There was never a definitive paper that demonstrated that these bodies were terrestrial in origin."

When Hoyle and Wickramasinghe published the results that freeze dried bacteria may be a component of stardust, the critics asked, "Where did all the bacteria come from?" We now have an answer to that question.

Millions of red giants, predating the formation of Earth, vaporized planets, moons, or comets and launched their microbe inhabitants into the starlight. Those microbes had the genetic information to maintain a habitable climate on a planet, survive radiation, and go dormant for millions of years. The sputtering release of comets, perhaps forced by periodic encounters with galactic objects, propelled the trapped microbes to seed new planets forming in the nebula around the sun and other star systems. Extraterrestrial microbes and organic molecules have landed on the surface of the Earth as part of the several tons of cosmic debris that enters the atmosphere every day.

For thirty-six years, between Bartholomew Nagy's publication of fossilized microbes in the Orgueil Meteorite and NASA's announcement of fossilized microbes in the Mars meteorite ALH84001, all evidence of extraterrestrial life had been dismissed.

Did NASA denounce the evidence to divert the public eye from possible errors of planetary protection during the Apollo missions to the moon? John Rummel, a marine biologist at Woods Hole and a former NASA planetary-protection officer, once told a journalist, "I don't worry about pathogens or things that would infect humans. I think my greatest nightmare is a flock of lawyers stopping a mission because no one has considered the possibility." Is NASA worried that its program will be damaged because of the public's fears over contamination by extraterrestrial organisms? Can they really be sure that extraterrestrial organisms have not had an influence on human health?

Perhaps, in the decades to come, the Mars science laboratory or a manned mission to that planet will resolve the issue. Meanwhile the public is tantalized and primed to accept the discovery of extraterrestrial life. Will the names of Bartholomew Nagy, Fred Hoyle, and Gilbert Levin be included in the legacy of that discovery? In more than four decades there has been no proof to eliminate freeze-dried microbes as a principle ingredient of stardust or to exclude the possibility that they ride to Mars and Earth on icy comets where, introduced to small ponds of water, they blossomed into the full richness of life. On the contrary, evidence supports the idea that, as of yet, undiscovered laws of nature and sources of information have orchestrated the formation of life throughout the cosmos. Or perhaps, as Fred Hoyle has suggested, life has always existed and always will.

ROGER HART is a former research professor at the College of Ocean and Atmospheric Sciences at Oregon State University, and was a member of the first American expedition to Mount Everest. He has worked as an exploration geophysicist in the rain forests of Ecuador and Brazil, had a glacier named after him in Antarctica, and lived and traveled in more than forty countries. Hart is the author of *The Phaselock Code: Through Time, Death and Reality: The Metaphysical Adventures of the Man Who Fell Off Everest (Paraview Pocket Books)*. This article is an excerpt from a work-in-progress called *The Conscious Earth*.

THE STRANGEST OF THE STRANGE
By Albert Rosales

Among the thousands of UFO reports and incidents collected from all corners of the Earth are a few reports that absolutely stand out from the rest, either as a result of their bizarre nature, or the actions of the UFO involved, or the appearance of the associated occupants. Though such reports are rare, they have been reported from around the world. Every UFO group or organization has its list of so-called "X-files," cases so bizarre in nature that they almost never come to light and remain hidden in the researcher's private files.

I wish to summarize a few of these strange and sometimes absurd cases, which are not widely known even within the UFO community. Most, if not all, of the cases I will be detailing are close encounters of the third or fourth kind.

Among those cases that I believe deserve the label of high-strangeness are those in which the witness or witnesses report the presence of two or more types of ufonauts or humanoids apparently cooperating amongst each other for an unknown purpose.

The following case is from France and, no, it is not from the 1954 UFO wave. Though rarely mentioned, it was listed in the last edition of the Humanoid Catalog (HUMCAT).

Location: Between Mairiuex and Maubeuge Nord France
Date: November 26, 1973. Time: 0100

A man and a woman in a parked car on the Canourge road, Mairieux, noticed a white metallic looking hemispherical object some 50-ft wide in the snow covered fields, 100 yards away. Presently a dark opening appeared in the object, from which six beings, of three different kinds, emerged. First were three small humanoids with large heads, four feet tall. They had protruding eyes with conspicuous whites, holes for a nose, narrow mouths, and bulging cheeks; their arms were long. They were dressed in tight one- piece suits of metallic appearance. Each carried a dark box six inches on a side whose upper surface bore a round white luminous "screen." They walked slowly, with stiff small steps, and fanned out as if searching for something. Gradually they approached the road, until within 50 ft of the witnesses. Behind them, nearer to the hemispheric object, stood two human figures about 6.5 ft tall, with light complexions and blond shoulder length hair, likewise dressed in tight fitting one-piece metallic suits. Closest to the door stood a squat figure, with long dangling arms, apparently covered with dark fur, "resembling a bear or great ape." When after about 10 minutes the small beings began to approach the car, the young woman became frightened and jumped out, slamming the door, and ran back to her own car which was parked nearby. At this, the man saw all the figures standing still, then the "animal" reentered the object, followed quickly by the two humans and then the three humanoids, which ran back with such long, swift strides that they looked as if they were "flying over the ground." The dark opening disappeared, and the UFO took on a brilliant metallic color, and rose vertically for 30 ft, then shot off westwards, becoming successively orange m luminous, bluish, and reddish before dwindling to a point. This all happened with such speed that the young woman observed only the recession of the luminous object. The witnesses did not seek traces in the snow. However, strange tracks in the snow were found later that morning by a Mrs. Michel and her children in the garden of their house in Maubeuge, 1.1 mile away from the incident. (Joel Mesnard & Jean Marie Bigorne)

Here is another example in which two types of beings were seen onboard a UFO.

Location: Near Tillamook Oregon
Date: September 27, 1989. Time: 16:20

A woman was alerted by her granddaughter to something unusual outside. She stepped out and was confronted by an object resembling an inverted toy top hovering just above the ground. It was 20 to 30 feet in diameter and had a flat bottom and a bright yellow-white light shining at both ends. The woman approached to within 30 feet of the craft and a door opened revealing a blond human-like entity of average height with fair skin and blue eyes, wearing a silvery coverall. The woman then noticed at a window next to the door a large hairy, Bigfoot type creature apparently seated and only visible from the chest up. The woman stared at the object and beings for a few minutes, and then the object suddenly vanished from plain sight. (*MUFON Journal*, 264, April 1990)

With so many so-called abduction reports from all over the world, many of the accounts involve the same sequence of events reported over and over again. But once in a while we run into a case that it is atypical for an abduction. The following is a curious example from Brazil.

Location: Curitiba, Brazil
Date: January 1978. Time: night

Claudia accompanied her young son Cristovao, to the elevator so he could go down to play. In the elevator they met a strange man who smiled at Cristovao. Later worried about her son not returning home early she went to ask the doorman about her son and he told her that he had not seen him get out of the elevator. They searched in vain for young Cristovao the rest of the night. Around the same time strange events were occurring in the apartment: objects were moving on their own volition and a sound similar to a "beep" was constantly heard. The next morning, around 0800, an employee at a local power plant discovered Cristovao sleeping on the grounds of the plant. According to Claudia, Cristovao was emitting a very strong odor and told her an incredible story about boarding a "rocket" that took him to a yellow moon; from there he was taken to an even larger "moon." There he encountered a man and a woman that appeared to lack mouths. The humanoids apparently inserted some items in Cristovao head and gave him rice and fish to eat and a reddish gaseous drink. In that place Cristovao saw other children. He was later placed on a small bed, covered with a blanket and allowed to sleep. He told his mother that they would one day return for him. She also discovered several marks on her son's skin that had not been there previously. He kept pointing at the region of the sky where he said the "yellow moon" had appeared. The strange paranormal occurrences around the house continued for a while and then abruptly ceased. (Pablo Villarubia & Mario Rangel)

Sometimes an abduction seems to be a brief sojourn into a kind of parallel reality, as the following case from Russia illustrates.

Location: Rostov-on-Don, Russia
Date: January 14, 1978. Time: 06:00A

Three 18-year old men, Mikhail Babkin, Nikolay Leontyev and Vitaliy Kravchenko were in a room at the local sports complex, "Oktyabryonok." They had been celebrating the passing of the old New Year with glasses of champagne and enjoying steam baths in the sauna and swimming pool, also eating mixed with some vodka. At 0600 the watchman proposed that the young men go home and accompanied them to the rear exit of the building, through a long corridor with concrete walls without windows. The corridor was located in the basement area near the pool's walls. They were walking along the corridor in the following order, the watchman walking ahead, followed by Leontyev, then Babkin, and Kravchenko. The corridor was very narrow. Suddenly Babkin seemed to trip, despite the narrow corridor and the obvious lack of reason. The smooth concrete floor had no potholes. However Babkin's left leg had tripped over some kind of "hole." He screamed and Leontyev turned around in amazement. He could not believe his eyes as he saw Babkin's shoulder penetrate into the concrete wall and in a moment Babkin's entire body vanished into the wall. He disappeared, apparently dissolving into the wall (!). The stunned witnesses began examining the wall with their hands looking for any doors or crevasses but their hands only touched concrete. Mikhail later told his friends that he had suddenly entered a small and dark room. To his left he could see an object, which resembled a medical examination chair. Across from him he could see a slightly opened door. There was a narrow window on the right wall of the room. He could see tops of trees entirely covered in dense green leaves and moving about in a strong wind. Babkin was amazed, it was in the middle of winter, but outside this "window" it appeared to be summer and broad daylight. Also a few seconds ago he had been walking in an underground corridor and here he was looking at a view of from a fourth story floor. Moving as if in a trance Babkin approached the slightly opened door and pushed it open. He then entered another room, also shrouded in gloom. There was a round platform on the ceiling that gave off a faint light and there were no windows in the room. A similar "medical chair" stood near the wall. He felt very lightheaded and moved about like a robot; he walked forward and opened another door, stepping into the strangest room yet. It was absolutely dark, with some bright areas visible in the inky darkness. The lights seemed to hypnotically influence Babkin. He became numb, unable to look away from the lights. Suddenly he noticed several black humanoid figures that appeared in front of him, faintly lit by the pulsating patches of light. Their heads appeared rectangular in shape. They were five of them and they stood unmoving in front of him. One of the humanoids, standing in the front was slightly hunched over and appeared to be working with some kind of device that gave off light. The device was not big, resembling a "corncob" with a pointy end, which was aimed directly at Babkin. The object emanated a very bright light but strangely it did not illuminate the surrounding area. Babkin then heard a male voice inside his head, which said, "This one?" Another voice, also inside Babkin's head answered, "No, not him." The first voice then said immediately, "Memory erasure is necessary." This phrase frightened Babkin terribly. He realized with deafening clarity that it was his memory that was going to be erased. Horrified, Babkin seemed to snap out of his confused state and ran out the door and suddenly jumped back into the corridor of the sports complex, screaming inarticulate remarks. He heard a door closed behind him with a loud slam, when he turned around the door was gone. His friends had been searching for him for about an hour, running across the complex in complete despair. But according to Babkin he had spent only five minutes in that other strange parallel world. (X-Libri UFO Russia & Alexey K. Priyma, *Unknown Worlds*, 1996)

This case is unknown in the West, but well known among ufologists in Eastern Europe where similar incidents have been recorded. It is difficult to classify such an event, which describes what appeared to be a totally alien environment beyond detection by our normal senses.

Some abductions are what I call permanent abductions. Of course, such abductions have to be witnessed by others in order to be reported, like the following example again from Brazil.

Location: Piranhas near Rondonopolis, Goias, Brazil
Date: January 19, 1978. Time: 17:15

Six young boys were playing soccer on a field when they saw a luminous disc-shaped object flying over the area. It flew at treetop level then stopped and descended to the ground without making a sound. Four of the boys ran terrified to their houses while two cousins, Manoel and Paulinho Roberto, remained behind. The children told their parents and a search for the two cousins ensued. Later, after midnight, a telephone call from the police alerted the family of Manoel Roberto that he had been picked up by an engineer, a Mr. Touro, in the nearby city of Rondonopolis, cold and hungry and looking for shelter. He said that as the object landed he and his cousin Paulinho also tried to run but were unable to move. They were then attracted towards the object. Inside the craft they found themselves in a large room where there was only a chair and a large button on the wall next to it. In the room there were also eight short humanoids, wearing reddish rubbery tight-fitting suits. Their faces were human-like. Both boys remained on the chair unable to move, until one of the short men approached and passed his hand over the side of the chair. Later the object landed in Rondonopolis and Manoel was let go by the humanoids. Around the same time there was a reported power outage in the area. His cousin Paulinho has never been seen or heard from again. His whereabouts remain unknown. (Guillermo Manuel Gimenez ONIFE-CEP)

The following is another example of a witnessed, permanent abduction from South America.

Location: Cajamarca, Peru
Date: December 26 1976. Time: 18:00

While numerous farmers were returning home from the fields, walking along the main road, they observed an intense violet light approach them from a distance of about 120 meters away. Ahead of the group were Candelaria Tucto Chilon and her young daughter. As everyone watch stunned the light seemed to transform itself into a metallic disc-shaped object the likes of which had been seen on numerous occasions in the region. The craft approached Candelaria and her daughter and without stopping it transformed itself into a bright violet light again, which seemed to envelope mother and daughter. The light then disappeared into the sky. Mother and daughter were never seen again. Three witnesses testified to the civil guard about the truthfulness of the incident. (*Mas Alla de La Ciencia*, 1991)

Here is yet another example, again from Brazil.

Location: Navegantes Beach, Santa Catarina, Brazil
Date: August 31 1974. Time: night

Antonio De Azevedo, an angler, was on the beach with his wife when they saw a discoid object with varicolored lights land close beside them. It was shaped like "two plates with the rims stuck together." The vivid lights temporarily "paralyzed" the observers. From the object emerged "three strange short beings wearing greenish spacesuits;" their faces "seemed to reflect the green color of their clothes." Conversing in a strange language, they quickly "examined" the angler and his wife, then seized the latter and took her into the object, which took off at incredible speed. (Gordon Creighton, *Flying Saucer Review*, v21, n2)

Apparently the woman was never seen again.
Another high-strangeness category in my point of view is instances in which a close encounter with an unknown craft or a humanoid results

in death or grievous injury to the witness or witnesses soon after the incident. The following example comes from Peru.

Location: Tingo Maria, Peru
Date: November 20 1968. Time: unknown

It was reported that in a jungle area a large disc-shaped object descended and came to rest on the ground near three boys who were playing in a nearby field. Curious, they approached the object and noticed two short figures standing next to it. One of the boys attempted to get nearer the object but he suddenly went unconscious. The two short beings signaled the other two boys to approach and to retrieve their fallen friend, which they did. The child was supposedly taken to a local hospital where he died, suffering from third degree burns. On the site an area of scorched brush was found. No other information. (Fabio Picasso)

While the consequences may not have been intentional on the part of any presumed UFO occupants, the following cases are worth noting.

Location: Pedrosa del Rey, Valladolid, Spain
Date: July 21 1975. Time: 19:00

Farmer Emiliano Velasco Baez was working his fields on his John Deere tractor in an area known as Parcel 21 when suddenly a strange sound attracted his attention. Thinking that the motor had been damaged, he was about to stop the tractor when he saw a bizarre looking object some 20 meters away and hovering only about 80 cm above the ground. The craft then began to slowly turn towards the witness. At this point he was able to observe it in detail. He described it as a metallic cylinder with a sombrero shaped cupola on top, and a V-shaped support on the bottom. He saw what appeared to be a window and a door on the object. The object's trajectory brought it within ten feet of the witness. At this point a deafening whistling sound invaded the area. While performing one of its turns the witness felt and saw a beam of light that apparently struck him and his tractor, drilling a perfectly round hole in the rearview mirror of the tractor. Now somewhat scared Emiliano accelerated his tractor and quickly drove away from the area. Years later, after suffering from numerous ailments that only began to afflict him after the encounter with the unknown object, Emiliano Velasco Baez died. His wife always attributed his death to the UFO encounter. (Iker Jimenez, *Encuentros, Historia de los Ovnis en España*)

The following case seems to suggest some type of radiation poisoning.

Location: Nildottie, South Australia
Date: Early 1979. Time: Evening

The two witnesses, Jack and Don, had been experiencing problems with their TV antenna being twisted around. The cause puzzled them. One evening after cooking a meal, the Venetian blinds went up and down. Both went outside to look and were approached by European-looking people. They appeared to be wearing woolen jumpers. There were both male and females. A bright light shone on them and both men felt calm. They were then taken over to a mound of gravel adjacent to which a craft was located. The men were taken inside. It was cold and the beings apparently agreed to escort them back to the house to get jumpers. They were not allowed to take food. They then returned to the object and it took off. As it rose they saw the TV antenna on the house below twist around. They could see across the Murray River as they rose up. Don, the younger of the two, was given strange, repetitive tests. Seven hours later they were returned. When a neighbor visited and found them confused, police were called in. The two men were taken to a local hospital. They seemed to be suffering from yellow jaundice and eye problems. Both men passed away within two years of the encounter. (Bill Chalker, *The Oz Files*)

The following case seems to have a direct connection between UFO activity and human deaths.

Location: Vila Gorete, Para, Brazil
Date: Beginning of September 1979. Time: Night

Near the banks of the River Tapajos several witnesses, including one Maria Lopes, reported seeing a large disc-shaped object descend and land silently in a wooded area near the river. From inside the craft two men and a woman came out who then proceed to approach a couple of possibly drunk and sleeping fishermen lying on the ground who offered no resistance. Lopes and other fishermen watched the scene from nearby, unable to move. In the morning they found both fishermen dead. On the chest area right above where the heart is, each man had dozens of needle-like objects inserted into the heart. Strangely, each man had about 5,000 cruceiros in their pockets. Panic swept the area and according to locals a strange luminous object appeared almost every night over Vila Gorete. It would then descend over the forest and land in a clearing. Other witnesses near Belem reported seeing a huge yellowish sphere flying overhead and one man reported three strange man-like figures wearing metallic bronze-colored uniforms walking on the banks of Lake Utinga. (Iker Jimenez "Las Luces de la Muerte" quoting Jorge Thor)

From 1976 through well into the 1990s, the area of Northern Brazil was flooded with numerous reports of UFOs that caused harm and injury to the witnesses. The activity is well documented in the official Brazilian Army report, "Operacion Prato" (Operation Disc or Plate).

Another type of report that should be considered as having very high strangeness content is reports of giant entities or aliens, which are not very common but are indeed dramatic. Here is one example from Spain.

Location: Tarifa, Spain
Date: September 1964. Time: 0230

The witness was walking back to his home alone on a path along the coast. As he neared his home on the cobbled road, he noticed a strange silence. His dogs that usually greeted him were nowhere in sight. As he turned a corner he caught sight of an enormous humanoid standing by the roadway next to a rock wall. The being was about three meters tall. The witness was stunned but strangely did not feel any fear. The humanoid wore a tight-fitting, scaly gray-colored diving suit. It was of normal build except for slightly narrow shoulders. The being stood there, looking out to sea. The witness was not able to see any clear details of the face or head area. The being then spoke in perfect Spanish, asking the witness if there were any fish factories in the area and if he was from around these parts. They stood and looked at each other for a few moments and then the witness continued on to his house and did not see the being's departure. He almost fainted as he arrived home. (J. J. Benitez, *La Quinta Columna*–The Fifth Column)

Or consider this fascinating encounter from Uganda in Africa.

Location: Between Kinyara & Kitanosie, Uganda
Date: 1995. Time: Night

The anonymous witness, while walking home on a road through the sugar cane fields, abruptly stopped by an unfinished airstrip and turned to his left. There stood a huge, red-colored winged creature with glowing blond curly hair and what seemed to be a halo effect surrounding his head. The sugarcane at the time had been left uncut for many years and stood about 16 feet tall. The "angel" was about 12 feet tall and the most beautiful creature that he had ever seen. The being appeared to have an additional set of ribs that were below his normal ribs, that is, about waist level. His legs were fur like and it stood upon hooves instead of feet. The two stood some 60 feet apart and just looked at each other for about five minutes. The being exuded a very bright light from its body and head, which gave a halo effect. The witness thrust his hand towards the being as a gesture of contact and at this point heard a message of a religious nature and of future warning for humanity, all in his mind. After the message, the "Red Angel" turned and his wings unfurled and trailed behind his body as he returned back into the sugar cane. The witness continued to walk towards home. About 150 yards further up the road the "Red Angel" appeared again, standing amongst the cane. The witness turned and faced him again, this time standing about 30 feet away. The being's face, although white, was glistening black as if in shadow. Soon the bizarre humanoid disappeared into the sugarcane field again. (Direct from the witness who requested confidentiality)

Other reports describe even more bizarre entities.

Location: Hollywood, Florida
Date: April 2003, Time: 0100

Two women came to the side of the South Florida gatehouse where "June" worked as a security guard. They said that there was something strange out by the curb, about 100 feet away, but they didn't know what it was. It was on the road just east of the driveway. The women were upset and seemed to think that something was very wrong. June instructed the women to wait in their car by the gatehouse while she went to investigate. If there were any problems they could call the police on their cell phone. June walked out to the curb and found sitting on it, curled up into a ball somewhat smaller than a beach ball, a strange "person." With her flashlight June could see a neck and a dark suit. Gently, June touched the figure and said, "Hello!" but there was no movement. Finally, as June touched the shoulder, a small woman suddenly unwound from the curled up ball position. She was about four and a half feet tall with very high heels on her shoes. She was dressed very well with beautiful jewelry, a leather purse, diamond-appearing earrings and long red hair that fell to her shoulders. Her face revealed very large brown eyes, a small nose and a tiny barely noticeable mouth. She appeared to be about 24 years of age and appeared to be afraid. June questioned her gently:

June: "What are you doing?"
Woman: "I m waiting."
June: "For whom?"
Woman: "A-a-a ride."
June: "Well, who is supposed to pick you up?"
Woman: "I don't know."
June: "Honey, come off the curb and stand next to me."
June put her hand around the little woman and noticed that she weighed maybe 70 pounds, had long arms and very long fingers.

Her pinstriped suit with a skirt looked as though it could have been made in the 1940s. Finally the woman looked at June and asked: "Where am I?"

June: "Well, we're on earth, and it's the fourth rock from the sun.

Woman: "Oh..."

June: "Can I do anything for you? Do you need the police?

Woman: "The who"?

June: "The Police."

Woman: "What do they do?"

June: "They might be able to help."

Woman: "No, I am all right. I am just going to wait."

June took hold of her and insisted she come with her to the gatehouse to talk for a while. But the strange woman insisted that she wanted to wait by the curb. At this she sat back down and curled up into a ball again. Reluctantly June returned to the gate where she found the other two ladies still waiting in their vehicle. June then called the police, which came around and spoke to the woman for 45 minutes but could not detain her. They told June that the woman did not have any identification on her, and no keys, but had some money and small papers with scribbles on them in her purse. They said that they had no reason to detain her and left. After the police left, June went out to check on the little woman but she had vanished into thin air. (*Miami Skyscan*, July 2003)

In 1973 there occurred an encounter in England that seemed to epitomize the term "high-strangeness" in its entire splendor. The tale is haunting, almost fairy tale like in nature.

Location: Sandown, Isle of Wight, England
Date: May 15, 1973. Time: 16:00

Fay, seven, with a boy about her own age, was on the golf links when they heard a wailing siren-like sound. They followed it through a hedge into a swampy meadow. The noise ceased. As they were crossing a brook by a footbridge, a strange figure came out from under the bridge. This person fumbled with a book, dropped it in the water, retrieved it, and then went with "a strange hopping motion, with knees raised high" to a metallic "hut" with no windows. The being was nearly seven feet tall and neckless. He wore a yellow, pointed, hood-like hat with a black knob on top and "wooden" antennae or horns on the sides, along with a green tunic with a red collar. "His face had triangular markings for eyes, a brown square of a nose and motionless yellow lips." Other round markings were on his paper-white cheeks, and a fringe of red hair fell onto his forehead. "Wooden slats" protruded from his sleeves and from below his white trousers. There were only three fingers on each blue-gloved hand and three toes on his bare white feet. The being carried from the hut a black-knobbed microphone into which he spoke (the children were now 50 yards away), saying "Hello, are you still there?"

Since his tone sounded friendly, they approached him. He then wrote in a "notebook," in a large hand, "Hello and I am all colors, Sam." Talking without the aid of a microphone – his lips did not move and his speech was unclear – he asked the children about themselves. They in turn asked about his clothes, which were all ripped, and if he were really a man. "No," he replied, with a chuckle. When they asked if he was a ghost, he answered "Well, not really, but I am in an odd sort of way." "What are you then?" they asked, to which he replied, "You know." He also said that he had no name, and "confided that he was frightened of people." At his invitation, the children crawled through a flap into his hut, which he told them he had "just made." It contained two levels. The lower, which "had plenty of headroom," was "wall papered" in blue-green and covered with a pattern of dials; there was an electric heater and simple wooden furniture. The upper level, less spacious, had a metal floor. He told the children that he fed upon berries, which he collected, and drank the river water after "cleaning" it. He said he had a "camp" in the mainland. Inside the hut he removed his hat to reveal round, white ears and sparse brown hair. Before eating a berry, he performed an "odd trick" with it; he placed the berry in his ear, where it disappeared and reappeared at one of his triangular eyes; "repeating the process, the berry traveled to his mouth." The children talked to this being for at least half an hour, then rushed across the golf links to tell the first man they met they had seen a ghost. (*BUFORA Journal*, v6 n5)

Each story seems stranger than the next. High strangeness, they call it. And every year more such stories are added to the pile, a very high pile. In fact, I just received one from Pennsylvania in which…

ALBERT SANTIAGO ROSALES was born in Cuba on a January 3, 1960 and as a boy in Cuba he saw things that could have been termed anomalous, or UFOs, but he had no point of reference as to what they were. He migrated to Spain in 1967, when there was a massive UFO wave there, then moved on to the USA in 1968. He enlisted in the U.S. Navy in the late 1970s and was there for four years as a Radioman with a top-secret clearance. He has now worked for local law enforcement (Miami Dade police) for almost 22 years. Yes, people do call 911 to report UFOs.

THE PERCH LAKE MOUNDS MYSTERY
By William Beauchamp

Perch Lake is located in Jefferson County, New York, in the north central part of the state. A century ago, along bluffs on either side of this lake, were more than 200 Indian mounds, some of which remain today. These symmetrically circular mounds were 20 to 30 feet in diameter, ranged in height from two to five feet, and had depressed centers with a diameter of about eight feet. The mounds often came in pairs--sometimes with intersecting walls--or in small clusters.

The mounds in New York are attributed to the Mound Builder culture. The term Mound Builders is used to describe Native North Americans from the Archaic, Woodland, and Mississippian period cultures who built these signature earthen mounds, apparently for burial, residential, or ceremonial purposes. The world's largest and best known ancient mounds site is the Newark Earthworks in Ohio, which are thought to be 2,000 years old; they range in height from three to 14 feet and once sprawled over four square miles. Another prominent example of early Mound Builder construction is located at Poverty Point in what is now Louisiana. The mound building cultures, whose earthworks some early white people thought resembled those of the ancient Britons and Gauls, lasted more than a thousand years and ranged over much of the eastern United States.

The Mound Builder culture is thought to have spread from the Ohio Valley to the Hopewell Indians of Western New York around 300 A.D. But the mounds at Perch Lake are quite unlike the mounds found in other parts of the state, which are quite small and simple in character. What were the Perch Lake mounds used for? They were not burial mounds and they don't appear to have been the foundations of circular lodges. So what were they?

This early, in-depth study of the "Perch Lake Mounds" was written by William M. Beauchamp more than a century ago and published in April 1905 by the New York State Museum in Albany in Bulletin 87 Archeology 10. *Some spelling has been modernized, such as height for hight. An update on the mounds follows this reprint.*

In all histories of Jefferson County, N. Y. there are slight notices of the curious mounds about Perch Lake. When Squier wrote his account of the antiquities of New York they had not attracted attention, for they were inconspicuous and remote from ordinary travel. Mr. F. B. Hough seems to have been the first to mention them, a few years later, and he said there were several at the mouth of Lowell Creek, Perch Lake, about 30 feet across and with depressed centers. No creek is now known by this name to the oldest inhabitants, but he probably meant Hyde Creek at the head of the lake, where there are yet a number. He added that there are some on Linnell's Island. In these were found pottery, burnt stone and charred corn. (*Hough,* p.10)

Linnell's Island is not in the lake, but is an extensive elevation in the great swamp west of its foot and north of the outlet, as shown in plate 1. It lies between two large streams and is now occupied by farms. Some mounds still remain on those owned by Messrs Gailey and Klock. No charred corn has been reported by any accurate investigator, and small coals may have been mistaken for this. Very little pottery has anywhere been found, but charcoal and burnt stone appear in all. In French's *Gazetteer* it is said that "in the vicinity of Perch Lake have been found several harrows, or sepulchral mounds." (*French,* p. 360) It would not have been surprising if some of the larger ones had had a secondary use for burial, being well adapted for it in such a region, but no evidence of this has yet been found.

Regarding these Mr. J. S. Twining wrote me in 1886 of a more extensive distribution of these mounds than has been given by others. He said:

> We have extensive vestiges of a much older race than those who built the forts and made the pottery. They are scattered along Black river, some 6 miles from

Copenhagen, and also on the hills back of Perch Lake, some 10 miles from Watertown, on the farms of John Gailey and A. Klock. On the latter are the largest and most perfect. They are the remains of camp bottoms, with a depression in the middle, with a true circle of camp refuse and burnt stones around them from 2 to 5 feet high, and with a diameter of from 20 to 30 feet. I have never found a piece of pottery in any of them, but plenty of flint chips. (*Beauchamp*, p.113)

Mr. D. S. Marvin made a day's exploration of the Perch Lake mounds in August 1886 in company with Messrs. Carter, Woodworth, and Woodard. The results he embodied in a paper read before the Jefferson County Historical Society, March 15, 1887, adding a few facts from the earlier explorations of Henry Woodworth and J. S. Twining. The lake is a small one, part of the shores high and rocky, but much more low and marshy. The mounds occur only on the higher part. The outlet is 6 miles long, and mounds have been reported near this. At the natural bridge, near its mouth, are extensive camp sites with abundant bone articles and fragmentary pottery. The most important part of Mr. Marvin's paper is quoted here as follows:

The objects that arrest our attention and interest us the most are the so called Indian mounds, observed along both shores of the lake, and more or less down the outlet. They are situated upon the bluffs overlooking the water, and reach back from the lake sometimes a hundred rods; they number some two hundred in all. These so called mounds are all round, usually from 50 to 90 feet in circumference; some of them double, and so near that their edges coalesce. They are elevated or raised above the summits of the hills they occupy from 2 to 4 feet. Where the land has not been cleared, ordinary forest trees of all ages are seen growing around and upon the mounds, ranging from yearling growths to trees several hundred years old. The debris usually

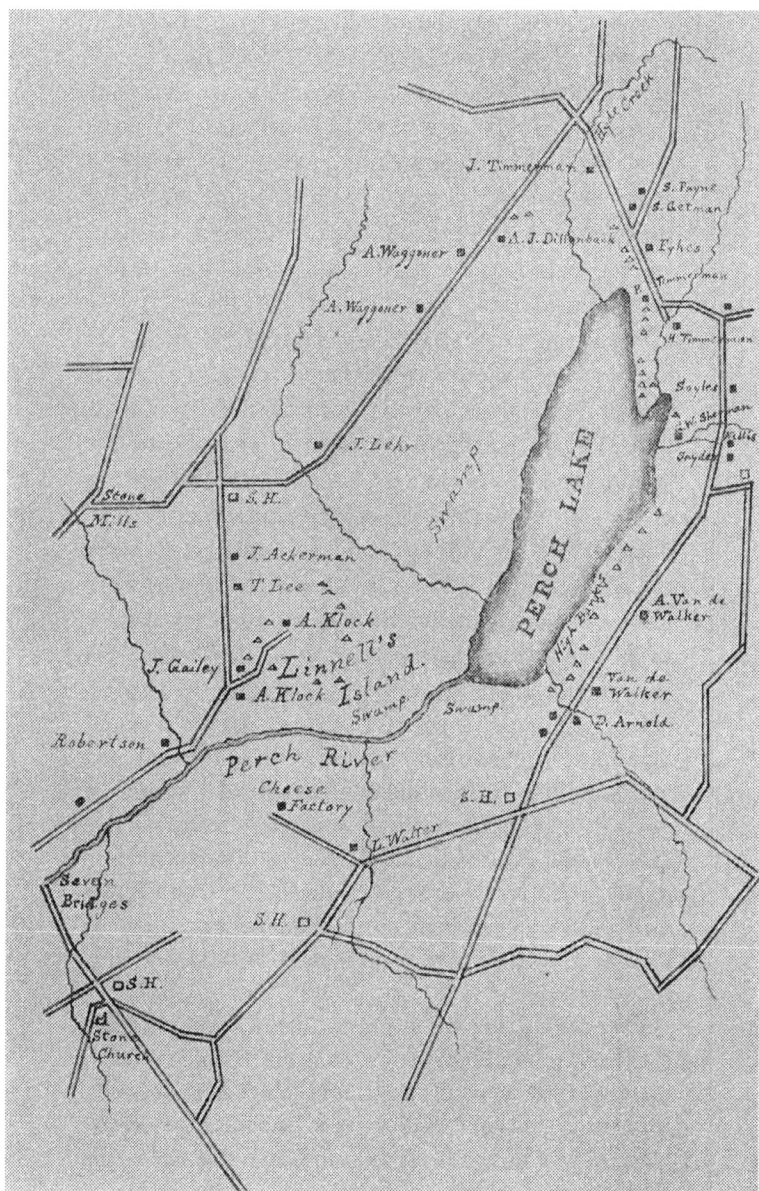

Plate: 1 Road map of Perch Lake and vicinity, from an atlas of Jefferson County. In this the lake differs much in outline and extent from the contour map but may have been fairly accurate at an earlier day. All remaining mounds on the east side are between the highway and the lake. In a few cases they are at some distance from the shore. Quite a space separates this long group from the one on Linnell's Island. It is said that some mounds were formerly near Seven Bridges, on Perch River.

THE PERCH LAKE MOUNDS MYSTERY   163

observed about old Indian villages is found buried in the soil, old bones and broken pottery; the organic remains though seem to have mainly rotted and gone to decay. The broken pottery observed was of the usual patterns, but it is only sparingly observed, for around some of the mounds none could be found. A few of the small mounds were flat topped, but the usual shape and appearance is a ring of earth, with a depressed or basin-shaped center.

In opening cross sections, or digging trenches from the outside to the center of the circles, as the centers are approached, remains of fires, charcoal, ashes, etc., were observed, sparingly though in the case of the largest mound. There was observed no disturbance of the soil below the level of the natural surface. The dirt of which the mounds had been constructed, is the common country soil, none of it seemingly brought from a distance, similar in character and composition to the soil of the adjacent land, made up of clay, sand and small fragments of the underlying limestone, belonging to the Trenton group, as near as I could determine from a cursory examination of the contained fossils, with here and there an occasional transported or drift pebble. The only observable difference was a darker color, caused by an increase of decayed organic matter and burned earth. No graves or human bones were observed. No lines of entrenchments were to be seen. Nor have there been any metal objects or utensils found.

The explanation of the phenomena observed here, that has seemingly puzzled several generations of white men, seems to be plain and simple. There is no necessity for bringing farfetched theories to explain the observed facts. Whoever has been to California and noted the singular rings of earth, with their basin-shaped centers, that are known to be the remains of the old rancherias of the Digger Indians, can readily see here in the close resemblances the original forms of Indian houses, belonging to the lower stages of barbarism, and probably a more or less universal style of house belonging to this stage of advancement, usually occupied only during the winter months, or generally deserted for nomad life during the warmer summer months. This style of house was constructed with a framework of poles set upon end and meeting at the top, and covered with dirt, leaving an uncovered space at the top to serve for the exit of smoke.

The writer once visited one of these dirt houses in California, large enough to hold several hundred people, but perhaps not larger than the remains of one of those observed at Perch Lake. Professor Thomas has described the remains of similarly constructed houses in Mississippi, Alabama and Georgia . . . I have also observed near Burrville, within a strongly fortified enclosure, circles of toadstools that had grown up from organic matters, old bones, etc., buried in the soil, showing that similar round houses once existed within fortified enclosures, but unfortunately both ditches and circles are now leveled by the plow. (*Marvin,* p.58)

I add some notes sent me in October 1901 by Mr. Henry Woodworth, one of the party mentioned, but whose conclusions are different. Both these gentlemen are careful observers:

I visited the mounds with Mr. Marvin and Clarence Woodard, and we spent one day at the lower end of the lake, on the south side. We found a very large mound on a ridge in the woods. Some large maple trees were in it. Distance from the lake was 10 or 15 rods. We did the most of our digging in that one, but we dug in others that were hollowed on top, as most of them are. We found but little to pay us for our labor. The ashes and coal that would naturally accumulate were very light. For that reason I think they were occupied only for a short time in the summer, for fishing and hunting. If they had been used to winter in, the accumulation would have been much more. I and my son dug some in the mounds on the Gailey farm at another time, but we found nothing to satisfy our curiosity. No shells were found in any of them by any one. We found no flint in any mounds. Mr. Gailey said some had been found, and stone pipes, but who has them I do not know. He says but little was ever found. I found no bone articles. We found some animal bones, but they were so decomposed that they easily crumbled to pieces. About the outlet and lower end of the lake are a number of mounds on the Gailey farm, of different sizes. Some are flat on top, but most have a depression in the center. Mr. Gailey said there are over 200 up the creek and around the lake. I think there are mounds below Mr. Gailey's, but I never visited the upper end of the lake.

He said there was no accumulation of burned stones in the mounds, probably meaning the small ones used in heating water. From this and the lack of pottery he concluded that no cooking, or but little, was done in them. Most of the many stones found show the action of fire, but they are usually of some size.

In a letter dated Aug. 4, 1900, Dr. Getman said:

We were at Perch Lake a few days ago, and examined the mounds that are found at each end of the lake. We were at the north end and along the banks of Hyde Creek. They are situated near the bank of the lake, extending upwards on to a high bluff of sandstone, and gravel of the same, along the banks of Hyde Creek. They are 25 to 30 feet across, 3 to 5 feet high, with a central depression of 8 to 10 feet in diameter. This depression is paved with the usual firestones. We saw one that was on a gravel bed, and had been partly removed. It was uniform in thickness, simply burned sandstone, gravel and black earth. The earth is different from the surrounding soil, being burned. We saw no pottery, bone, or anything that would give us a clue to the builders. Hough says broken pottery and bones are found there. This I think a mistake. Some have been dug to the center, and we were informed they had found flint and stone implements. There was only one that showed evidence of large timber growing from the site. We counted 15 in a piece of woods, and the trees (maple) were mostly small that were growing on the banks.

In a recent history of Jefferson County the mounds at the north end of the lake are again mentioned, but with little additional information save that of partial location. The editor says that at the lake 8 or 10 mounds are on the lands of George W. Sherman and Alonzo Van DeWalker 10 or 15 rods from the shore. They are circular, 2 or 3 feet high, 2 to 4 rods in diameter, and with the central holes 2 feet deep. The largest is said to be on the Sherman farm, near the ruins of the old La Farge mansion. (*Emerson*, p.738)

There are two large groups north of any of these, and but one mound was observed by me over 40 feet in diameter. The fine pair in front of the old mansion are by no means of the largest size, either in height or width.

Before adding notes of personal observations to these, it may be well to take notice of some kindred groups on the north shore of Lake Ontario, which I had planned to examine some years since. Mr. Thomas C. Walibridge read a paper "On some Ancient Mounds upon the Shores of the Bay of Quinté," Mar. 3, 1860, which was printed in the *Canadian Journal* for September of that year. These mounds had then been locally known as artificial for 50 years, but no account had been previously published. Commencing at Rednersville they could be traced along the bay about 8 miles to Massassaga point. This space, with the islands of Big bay, included about 100 distinct mounds, but others could be seen at intervals from the eastern to the western end of the Bay of Quinté. Others were reported at one place on the River Trent. Mr. Wallbridge said:

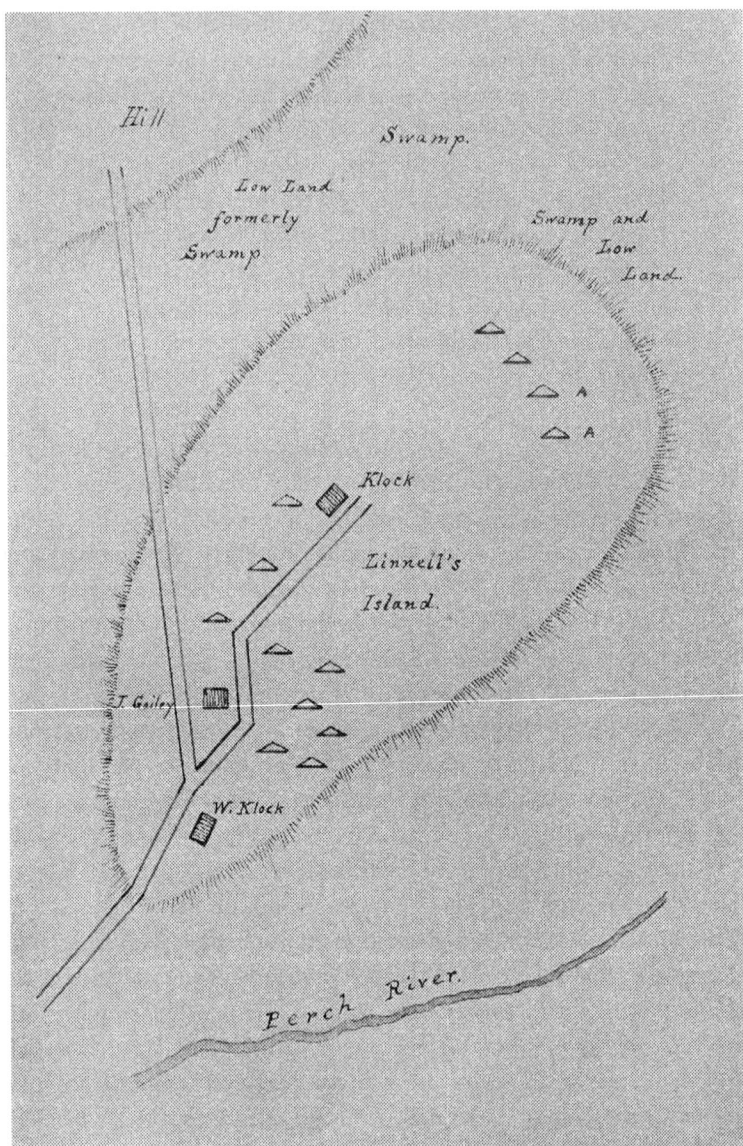

Plare 2   A sketch map of Linnell's Island by Dr. Getman, showing the general arrangement of mounds observed on the Klock and Gailey farms in 1903. This terrace is southwest of Perch Lake, and was formerly surrounded by swamps, showing a higher stage of water in the lake in earlier days. This subsidence has greatly changed the outline of the lake.

As far as has yet been ascertained, there is but one class or form of mounds in this part of the country, and the truncated cone is the shape they assume. In size they vary from a diameter at the base of 30 to 50 feet, to a diameter at the apex of 12 feet. Each mound has a shallow basin or circular depression upon its summit, which, whatever be the size of the work, has a diameter of 8 feet; and no mound under my observation possessed an altitude of more than 5 feet. It is a remarkable peculiarity of these works, that in almost every instance they occur in groups of two, and at irregular distances the one group from the other. Irregularity is likewise observable between any one mound and its fellow, these being sometimes found in juxtaposition, and again from 50 to 100 feet asunder. The two of the same group are always of one size. With respect to the surrounding country they are situate[d] apparently without design, now at the foot of a commanding hill, then halfway down the side of a bank, and again so near the shore that in several instances they have been destroyed by the action of the water. Twice they have been found in very low or swampy ground, and in those cases they occur singly. (*Wallbridge*, p.111)

He opened five of these at Massassaga point in August 1859. A cut was made 33 feet long, 2 feet wide and 3 feet deep, to the original surface. Under a few inches of mold was a heap of broken gneiss, conforming to the outer shape of the mound. The stones varied from 1 to 20 pounds each, but those forming the bottom of the basin were the smallest of all. Some showed the action of fire, but there were no traces of this in the mound. In making a cross-section some fragments of birch bark and bone were found above the stones. He said:

The other mounds examined agreed in all particulars of construction with that above described, excepting in one pair where it was evident from what remained that the inside margin of the basin of each mound had been surrounded with flat stones placed vertically and touching at their edges, as if designed to prevent the earth falling into the hollow. Similar stones, perhaps used for the same purpose, were observed lying near most of the other mounds in this vicinity.

He thought these had been displaced by diggers, and added:

In several instances the builders have been forced, from the nature of the surrounding country, to carry their material from a distance, but to obtain the usual covering of mold for the pair of mounds last mentioned they have bared the smooth underlying rock of its scanty soil, in a well defined circle about the works. The use of broken gneiss for a building material, to the almost entire exclusion of limestone, is a noticeable feature.

Limestone was most easily procured, but I think its change by fire may have made it objectionable. Large trees grew on some mounds, one oak stump being 8 feet around.

So far the likeness to the Perch Lake mounds is that of external form, size and situation, with a tendency to pairs. The interior differs in the character and arrangement of the stones, and the absence of coals. Similar ones were examined later, but one was of a sepulchral nature. This was excavated from the center to the natural surface. Some of the diagrams made are here partially reproduced.

Plate 10 figure 3, shows a section of the mound in which skeletons were found, with general features of the construction of all. In this appear the interior stones, the overlying soil and the central depression. Figure 2 shows the position of some articles found, and the central chamber. Ground was broken at 10 and a little below the surface was a flat, horizontal limestone, with fragments of human bones and birch bark, and a bone awl 8 inches long. These were probably from intrusive burial.

Another flat stone was found 2 feet from the surface, with three human skulls underneath, in a rude box of flat limestones. Many of the remaining bones were found, and five well preserved crania were secured. One skeleton at 6 was in a sitting position, with a pile of articles by it. Among these was the upper part of a bone comb, several teeth of the same, a unilateral bone harpoon, and three long shell beads. These articles do not indicate a high antiquity, and are much like those of New York. The burial was clearly intrusive.

A sketch of this interesting group has been given because it is little known, and partly because, being not far distant and in a very similar situation, it may have some relation to those of Perch Lake. The latter seem to have gradually increased in height; according to Mr. Wallbridge the former would seem to have been of nearly the same size from the beginning. This hardly seems probable, nor is it likely no fire was used in them, judging from what is found elsewhere. I saw no ashes in those of Perch Lake, and in some cases the coals were so blended with the soil as to be hardly distinguishable.

In the spring of 1901 I visited Perch Lake, where the old La Farge mansion once stood, at a considerable distance north of a large stream which enters the lake on the east side. Quite a point extends into the lake near this, back of which is a rocky bank, and thence the land rises eastward in low and broad terraces. On the greensward of one of these, not far from the bank, two of these mounds are conspicuous, one being a little above the other, and the edges meeting. At this spot they are the only ones in sight, and both have the characteristic circular form and depressed center. A little digging has been done in each, but this has affected the appearance very little. Though a little shaded they are practically in open ground. They are not of the largest size. The upper and eastern one has an extreme breadth of 34 feet, and an inside diameter of 14 feet from the interior slope. This is about 2 feet deep, within and without. The western one is of the same outside height, and is 32 feet across the base. The inside width is 17 feet, and the depth 3 feet. Some digging has been done in the center. The disturbed earth is black, containing burnt stones, but there are no signs of organic or artificial remains. Not far away there are many spots where the flat rocks form the natural surface, and about these the spring saxifrage was abundantly

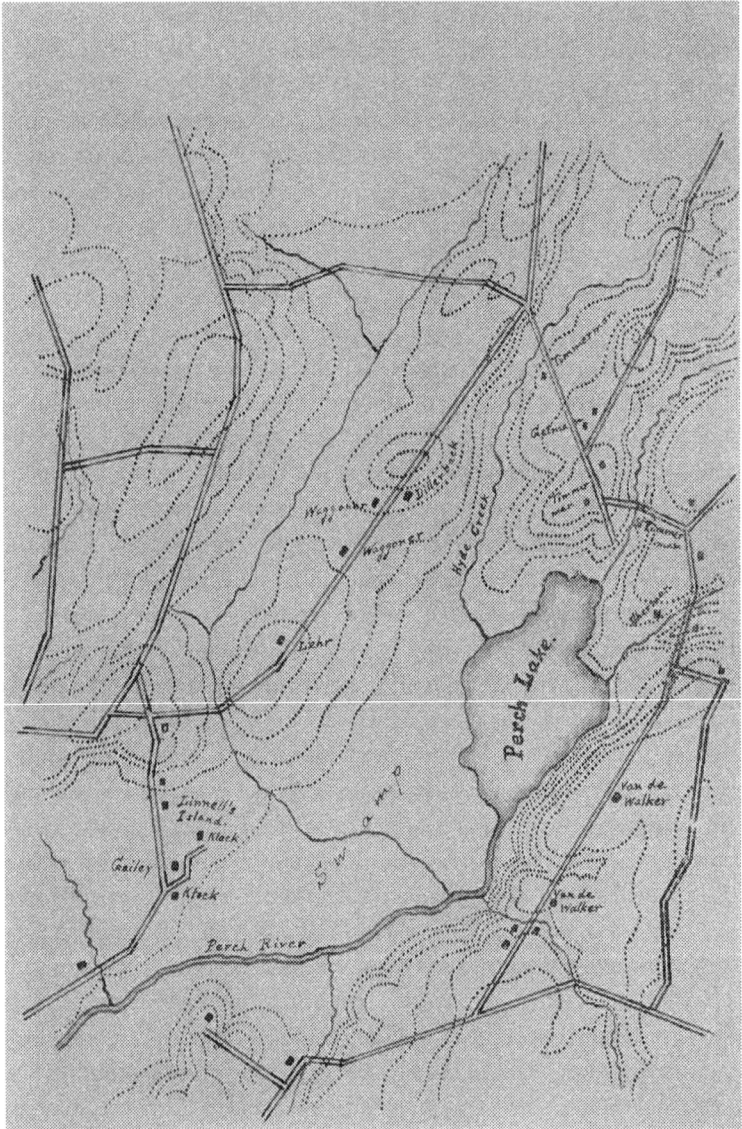

Plate 3 Contour map of Perch Lake and vicinity, showing numerous low terraces in the thin soil. In many parts these terraced rocks are nearly or quite bare. On the southeastern shore of the lake the slope is quite abrupt. On the west shore the extensive swamps, separating the cliffs from the lake, probably always hindered much occupation, but the proximity of the river to Linnell's Island made that a desirable residence.

in bloom. The low, symmetric mounds themselves formed a pleasing feature of the scene, full in view from the modern ruins as the land descended toward the lake. The spot is so convenient and beautiful that one might have expected to find more there, but for the evident tendency to place them in pairs or small groups.

It was late in the morning, and no satisfactory photographs could be obtained from lack of shadows. At a subsequent visit many mounds were examined in the rain, and others in the depths of woods and undergrowth. Many sketches were made, some of which are here given, but in no place could the camera be used to any great advantage.

A second visit was made in the middle of September 1901. A map of the vicinity had been secured, on a scale of a mile to the inch, and the general grouping will appear on this, shown on plate 1. As there was no special plan in the location of these structures, no necessity is felt for more exact details. They were placed where personal or family taste or convenience required. No rule appears in this except ease of access to the lake or streams. Some were on quite elevated land; others on broad hummocks, surrounded by marshy spots but little above the lake. In a few cases they were on the high banks above rocky streams, at some distance from the shore. The unpropitious weather prevented a personal examination of those at the south end.

As far as I could ascertain there are none now remaining on the west side of Hyde Creek and northwest side of Perch Lake. The lake may once have been higher than now and thus larger, but this did not affect the situation of the mounds, nor their probable age. Beginning on the west side of Hyde Creek a long line of cliffs runs parallel with the present shore toward the southwest, and between these and the lake is a broad expanse of swampy land, well covered with trees. No one could have lived in this swamp, nor was access to the shore through it in the least easy. I examined the undisturbed land at the top of these cliffs for a long distance, without finding a trace of aboriginal life. Every favorable indication was carefully examined, but nothing appeared. There may have been obliterated dwellings in the cultivated land farther back, but this is not probable. The swamp was an undesirable barrier to the lake.

THE PERCH LAKE MOUNDS MYSTERY   173

Farther north, on the west side of Hyde Creek, the case was different. That stream came fairly near the rocky uplands, affording an easy passage to the lake. Accordingly a few mounds were reported there, though none seem to remain. Certainly they were few. I was told of two mounds leveled by my informant on the A. J. Dillenbeck farm in 1901. These were 5 rods west of the swamp and 30 rods from the lake. In plowing there he found a broken flint knife, a fragment of pottery and a pottery rim, all of which he gave me. From the character of the rim I think there is an error of location. These were all the mounds of which I could learn on that side.

Mr. S. Getman said that he found a celt near two mounds he plowed up on the south part of his farm, at an early day, on the higher terrace east of the creek. I found no existing mounds as far north as this. A celt and arrowheads were reported from two mounds destroyed in 1900, on the upper terrace of the Timmerman farm. These had disappeared. The dual arrangement may be observed in all these mounds. It is probable that many mounds have long disappeared from this higher cultivated land. Those remaining are on the stony lower terraces. Commencing south of the Getman farm they extend along the shore to a stream called Ruff's Creek by some. South of this swampy lands again appear by the lake. This eastern shore is mostly high and rocky, rising thence in terraces, and the mounds appear here and there all the way. Some mounds may have escaped my attention in the undergrowth on the Van de Walker farms.

A medium sized mound was opened on the farm next south of S. Getman's. Plate 4 shows this, on the second terrace east of Hyde Creek and not far from it. It is 30 feet across and 2 feet high, with a broad central depression. A rectangular fireplace in the center was 8 feet across and edged with upright flat stones. This went down 2 feet below the present surface, the earth having been removed for the fireplace, and cast back as a foundation for the ring. Plate 12, figure 2, shows the surface plan. A is the outer slope, B the top of the ridge, C the inside slope, D the fireplace edged with stones, which is not an invariable feature. There were many coals in the black earth, no ashes and no vestige of anything else. There were many large stones. A trench was carried through to the original surface, and shorter

Plate 4 Medium sized mound on the second terrace east of Hyde Creek, and not far from it. The depression in the center of this is characteristic of nearly all the mounds near the creek and lake, and excavation showed the original rectangular fireplace bordered with flat stones. Like nearly all others, it is in open woodland. The extreme width is about 30 feet. A plan of this appears on plate 12.

cross-sections were made. A little southeast was another of similar size, rather flat and not prominent.

Another, farther south, is near the north line of the Timmerman farm. This is about 36 feet across and 2 feet high. It is flatter than most on top, but shows the usual depression. Small trees are growing on it, and there are some large stones along the edge. They may have been dug out of it, for most mounds have a few such stones. Plate 5 shows this.

A mound on the Timmerman farm has a large hemlock stump on it, and some small trees. It is a continuation of a low ridge, so that its exact dimensions are modified by this. As measured it is 28 feet wide by 2 feet high. The hemlock stump might show how old it must be, but not how old it might be. In these descriptions the general course is from north to south. A low ring, 19 feet across and on the same farm, tends to show that growth in height and width was slow, and by removals of matter from center to circumference; possibly by additions without. The depression is 8 feet across, but it was not noticed whether there was an enclosed fireplace. Plate 6 is of this. Another, west of the fence and this, is broad and low. Still another small one is on the lower terrace, not far away. Both these are northwest of the next.

A high mound on the edge of the upper terrace, and just west of the fence which crosses it, was not measured across, but is 3 feet high and with a deep central depression. A large stump is on the south side of this. Part of its effect is lost from its surroundings. There is an obscure one on the lower terrace a little west. Another low one with a wide and deep depression is on the same farm, and is shown in plate 7. It is about 21 feet wide, the height being usually in proportion to the width, and is an excellent example in its symmetry.

On the same farm is another 27 feet wide and 2 feet high, having a deep depression. A small one is just west of this, and perhaps related.

Another is 30 feet wide and 2 feet high, having a depression. There are some large stones outside of this. As the mound rose and the ring grew, it may have taken in loose boulders around, which had no relation to it. There is an obscure one north of this, and near a shanty in the woods. One on the south side of the shanty was 2 feet high.

A gravel bed, which has been opened in the woods, was cut through one of these mounds, in such a way as to give a good exposure. The bed reached above the mound on the east or upper side, the mound terminating a ridge, and nothing is seen in the exposure there. Another cut has been made in the mound below. At the base is coarse gravel, in its natural condition. Over this is a stratum of black earth, 3 feet deep and about 27 feet wide. The top and the extremities of the mound remain. Nothing was found in obtaining the gravel, nor was anything discovered in our farther digging. Not far from this, by the fence on the upper terrace, was another large one.

The finest mound on the Timmerman farm is near its southwest corner, in an open field and near the head of Perch Lake. It is 33 feet

Plate 5 A larger mound near the north line of the Timmerman farm. This is about 36 feet across from the extreme points of the slope, which is always gentlest near the edge and more abrupt as it approaches the center. This mound is less depressed in the center than most of those on that side of the lake.

wide and about 5 feet high. Plate 8 is of this. It is at the foot of a bold hillside, and itself on high ground. Digging had been done there, and the Rev. Mr. Scott is said to have obtained pottery and other things in 1901. We dug but little, and found nothing. Other low mounds were near toward the lake, and there is a large flat one quite a distance north. South of this group is low land for some distance, crossed by a rapid stream.

Leaving this stream and the low land the woods on the Sayles farm are reached, where there are many evergreens and a rocky shore along the lake. In these dark woods are other mounds. One is near the north end, and has its east side more elevated than the other, apparently from the slope of the land. This has quite a deep depression, and is of the usual size. A low and broad one is north of this, and two smaller ones south. Another large one is farther southwest. The depression is deep.

South of these woods is lower land and a brook, both north of the large point. A fine mound is on a low bluff in this bay. There are several mounds not far off. One is on the low bank near the shore; another south of this on a knoll or slightly higher land. Another, beyond the last and on the lake side of a knoll, has a very deep and large depression, 13 feet across. There is another at the south end of this ridge, and another in the low land east. Two are on the lower bank farther south, and there is a confluent group at the north base of the high terrace on which the La Farge mansion stood. The situation of these in these low lands is singular, though some of them are dry enough, and the spot is unusually sheltered.

South of the brook, as the large point is turned, there appear deep depressions and slight rings of an undecided character, and then come the two fine mounds in front of the ruined La Farge mansion, already described. Plate 9 shows the upper and larger one. South of this is low land, through which a large stream enters the lake. Beyond this creek no mounds appear for nearly half a mile, though some have probably been destroyed. Then one with a deep and broad depression appeared on a high bluff in the edge of the woods. It was about 27 feet across. High rocks here fringed the lake, with terraces above, on which was much undergrowth.

Nearly a quarter of a mile beyond was a doubtful one, not having a complete circle, and a similar one was on the edge of a knoll beyond. It is difficult to estimate distances while looking for mounds in thick woods, and it may be another quarter of a mile to a large and fine one on the second terrace. This was 27 feet wide, 2 feet high, and has a depression of 3 feet in the center. As before observed, it was usual to dig out the center in beginning these mounds. Not far away are two large ones, close together on the high bluff above the lake. Another just beyond is 36 feet wide, and the depression is 16 feet across. Another obscure one is farther south near the high bank of the lake. Between this and the cottages and boathouses beyond, is one 36 feet wide, 3 feet deep inside, and 2 feet outside.

A stream enters the lake at the boathouses. South of this and east of the shore is a large and high mound in which digging has been done. In the freshly turned earth no vestiges of early occupation could be seen except black earth and burnt stone. This mound is about feet high and 40 feet across. Common pottery was found in small camps by the shore. Beyond this is another low mound. Probably some in these woods were not observed.

After leaving the woodland the swamp is soon reached, and some mounds may have been obliterated in the open fields. North of the swamp flows a small rocky stream through these fields. On the brow of the upper terrace, on the north side of this is the largest and deepest mound I saw, measuring 45 feet across. Another is close beside this on the east, and another on higher ground still, in the rear of these and toward the road. On the south side of the stream, farther down and overlooking the water from a high bank, is another small but deep one under a tree. It is a pretty situation.

A large mound is near a shanty in the sugar camp, toward Ruff's Creek. This is 40 feet across and 3 feet high. A good deal of digging has been done there, but seemingly without results. A smaller one is near the shanty. This ended the explorations on that side of the lake. The oldest inhabitant knew of nothing taken from mounds south of the La Farge mansion. In all 54 mounds were observed, and 6 obliterated ones reported, or 60 in all. Other unobserved or obliterated mounds might much increase this number, but it is not likely to reach the higher estimates made for the whole territory.

At the north end of the lake is one spot deserving of a few words, and yet probably not connected with the general subject. In the edge of the swamp at the northeast angle of the lake, is an immense mass of rock which can be reached by a boat. In some of the depressions of this rock are many small flint chips, showing that it was a favorite spot for arrow makers. What weapons the makers of these mounds used is uncertain, but it is probable that the visitors to Squaw Island, as some call it, were of another people. The spot commands a view of nearly the entire lake.

Dr. A. A. Getman and Oren Pomeroy, of Chaumont, kindly made a close examination of the group I could not visit and with much the same results. Both are experienced and careful observers, and for this reason I give Dr. Getman's account, written Nov. 6, 1901.

Plate 6 A low and small mound on the Timmerman farm, shows the usual formation, but at noonday it might be passed unobserved. Early or late in the day its character is clear. Being in the incipient state it is but 19 feet across.

He wrote:

> We went to Linnell Island today. It is a limestone terrace, surrounded by lowland and swamp. . . Mr. Gailey says the island contains about 500 acres, with three farms at present. The soil is clay and a gravelly loam, with abundant outcroppings of rock (Chazy limestone). From the map you see the mounds dot the crest of the terrace all around the island; some at least 3/4 of a mile apart. Some of them appear to be built on the rock. In fact we dug the center of one down to see that it was started on the solid rock. We dug on this one near the barn. It had no central depression. We dug the center to the bottom; pit 4 feet square; then commenced at the edge on the south, and opened to this pit. There are less stones and more soil than at

the head of the lake, but we found lots of large hard heads, 8 to 12 inches across, about halfway from the edge to the center. All were burned. The depth was 2 to 4 feet from circumference to center. There were streaks of very dark earth and charcoal. Some of the charcoal was small limbs, 2 to 4 inches long, by 1 inch through. Three of the mounds have been removed for road building. They appear to make excellent roads. (These are marked A, A on the map, plate 2.) We saw some recent plowing which exposed three more. They were near those removed.

We looked over the three that had been used for roads. They had been only partially removed. The manner of working had been to plow the soil loose and shovel on the wagons; three men to *beam* the plow. In the plowed field some were smoothly plowed; on others the plow ran out. We found in the one near the house of J. Gailey, marked S, a skull and teeth of a muskrat, badly decayed, and a piece of broken stone that looked as if used for a nut stone. That is absolutely everything, except burned stones of all descriptions, charcoal and dirt; unless a few pieces of reddish crumbly pieces of stones were paint stones. S also shows some excavated mounds.

We looked over the plowed field, pawed over debris of the road mounds, and looked over the road that the stones were used on – a private road to the Kiock farm.

How many mounds there are I have no idea. We counted about 20, but there have been and are many more. I think, as a general thing, that they are smaller than those at the head of the lake, and of less depth. Mr. Clarence Galley claimed to have found two arrows when working the road business, but could not produce the find. It is very perplexing that no authentic relics can be found and handled. Pomeroy says the mounds are similar to the one we saw on Fox Island; that is the contents, stone, soil, etc.

Mr. R. D. Loveland, of Watertown, found a few small fragments of pottery in the large mound near the boathouse, but did not preserve them, as he obtained larger pieces of the usual types near the shore, where these might be expected. Had none been found elsewhere those in the mound might be thought intrusive. A clay pipe was also found near the shore.

In the *Bulletin of Natural History of New Brunswick* for 1884, p.14, Mr. G. F. Mayhew gives his ideas of how such hut rings were gradually raised. I infer that these might have been well known there, but am not certain on this point. He supposed that in some circular lodges moderate cleanliness was preserved, not by removing refuse altogether, but by drawing it back and filling in the center with fresh gravel. A constant repetition of this would preserve the circular form and the central depression as the mound rose above the surface. Bone needles found near the edge he thought had been stowed at the back of a couch. Pottery was much like that found elsewhere. Arrowheads were made by the fire, few flakes being seen out of doors. Most ordinary aboriginal implements were found.

This general mode of elevation reasonably accounts for the form and growth of the Perch Lake mounds. A pit was made in the center for the fire, and a large circle was thrown up at the edge of the lodge to carry off water. A slope from this to the fireplace gave an easy position to the reclining people within. It was necessary to remove or rake the embers away, and the edge gradually rose. To make it cleaner it was as easy to bring in a fresh supply of dirt as to carry accumulations away. In all this there was a natural overflow which enlarged the borders of the mound. The original fireplace was all the time retained, and so the largest mounds are the deepest.

Mr. Harlan I. Smith suggests a likeness in these to some he recently examined on the Pacific coast, and I give plate 10, figure 1, to illustrate this point. In his explorations he found that up to a recent date the Thompson River Indians made huts of this kind. In this section *a* is an excavation in the ground, which increased the height of the interior of the lodge, and supplied material for its covering. Around this excavation an arch *b* was raised, resting on the surface *c*. This arch had a frame of saplings and branches underneath, covered with dirt and sods. In the center of this strong frame above an opening, *d*, was left. This was reached by a primitive ladder, *e*, made of a notched pole which gave strength to the roof. This was the only means of ingress or egress for light, smoke and Indians. He found one still standing in a dilapidated condition, but observed the remains of many. When the roof fell in, a low mound was formed, with a marked central depression. These would probably differ from the Perch Lake mounds in the size of this depression, the height of the circle, and the evidences of fire throughout. The latter were probably simple tepees, pitched from time to time on the same spot, but not continuously occupied. The accumulation was gradual, but earth might have covered the lower part of the wall.

In his report on *Mound Explorations,* Prof. Cyrus Thomas described some mounds of this class closely connected with larger mounds in the Welch group, Brown County, Illinois. The group "consists of six mounds, and a number of small saucer-shaped basins surrounded by low, earthen ridges, doubtless the sites of' ancient dwellings or wigwams." (*Thomas,* p.118) He adds that "the dwelling sites vary considerably in size, some being as much as 70 feet in diameter, and some of them 3 feet deep in the center after 50 years of cultivation." In describing those on the Big Mary River, Ill., he adds something on their situation and origin:

> These are situated upon a flat topped ridge, about 30 feet higher than the creek bottoms. They are low, with the usual depression in the center, but the outlines are rather indistinct. Mr. Gault of Sparta, who has long resided here, states that when he first moved to this section, the Indians lived in houses or wigwams which, when decayed, left such remains as these. They hollowed out a shallow circular cavity in the surface soil, then, standing poles around the margin of this basin, brought them together at the top, and having covered them with bark or other material – in other words having constructed wigwams of the usual circular form – covered them in whole or in part, specially the lower

Plate 7   A low mound, on the same farm as that shown on plate 6, which is but 21 feet across. Though not large, it is very symmetric. The central depression is wide and deep.

portion – with earth. He also said that after a camp was abandoned and the wood rotted away, it left these rings of earth. (Thomas, p.141)

In one enclosure near Lakeville, Stoddard County, Missouri, he says,

Nearly the whole space between the walls is occupied by the hut rings or circular depressions. They are of the usual size, 20 to 50 feet across, and 1 to 3 feet deep. (*Thomas*, p.174)

These contained, ashes, pottery, etc., and he mentions no ridges. In another group the rings varied from 21 to 34 feet across. In another large group we get a more definite idea of the elevation, a feature in which most of these seem to differ from those of Perch Lake. This is at Beckwith's fort, Mississippi County, Missouri. After describing the enclosure he says of the hut rings:

> These almost cover the remainder of the area, the
> only open space of any considerable size being the
> 200 feet square just east of the large mound. They
> are not confined to the natural level of the enclosure,
> as some are found on the level tops of the mounds.
> They are circular in form, varying from 30 to 50 feet
> in diameter, measuring to the tops of their rims, which
> are raised slightly above the natural level. The depth of
> the depression at the center is from 2 to 3 feet. Near
> the center, somewhat covered with earth, are usually
> found the baked earth, charcoal, and ashes of ancient
> fires, and around these and beneath the rims split bones
> and fresh-water shells. Often mingled with this refuse
> material are rude stone implements and fragments of
> pottery. The similarity in the size, form, and general
> appearance of these depressions and earthen rings to
> those of the earth lodges of the abandoned Mandan
> towns along the Missouri river, leaves no doubt that
> they mark the dwelling sites of the people who formerly
> occupied this locality. (*Thomas*, p.187)

These mere depressions illustrate but one feature of the Perch
Lake mounds, and we have a closer correspondence in those described
by Prof. F. W. Putnam in the 11th report of the Peabody Museum,
and quoted by Mr. Thomas. They were some observed by the former
in Tennessee, and thus described:

> Scattered irregularly within the enclosure [the earthen
> wall which enclosed the area] are nearly one hundred
> more or less defined circular ridges of earth, which are
> from a few inches to a little over 3 feet in height, and of
> diameters varying from 10 to 50 feet... An examination
> of these numerous low mounds, or rather earth rings,
> as there could generally be traced a central depression,
> soon convinced me that I had before me the remains

of the dwellings of the people who had erected the large mound, made the earthen embankment, buried their dead in the stone graves, and lived in this fortified town. (*Thomas,* p.662)

Professor Thomas adds that these hut rings "are seldom, if ever, met with except on the site of an ancient village, and often one that was defended by an enclosure." This again differentiates the western and southern forms from those of New York. The latter are scattered or in very small groups, have the depressed center very little below the natural surface, are usually of considerable height, show the action of fire, but rarely contain ashes or relics of any kind, have no bones or shells, and the earth of which they are composed has been gradually gathered from year to year. With all this difference there is an unmistakable likeness, and no hesitation is felt in calling them the foundations of early lodges.

Two things naturally arrest attention. There are no bones or shells revealing the food of the inhabitants, though the conditions are favorable for their preservation. Most of them contain no articles made by man. The favorite fresh-water clam of the New York Indians was *Unio complanatus.* It is so widely distributed that it probably occurs in Perch Lake, though I observed none along the shores. If it is not found there that part of the problem is solved. But these aborigines were there for the fish of the lake, as well as for the game in the woods. Their homes had an easy access to the water. Why are no bones of any kind found under these conditions? The Iroquois sites yield them abundantly. It may be due to an Algonquin superstition. All will agree that these were not Iroquois homes, for they rarely used the circular lodge, which the Algonquins commonly preferred. There were differing tastes and beliefs of other kinds. The Iroquois left bones of every description on the ground. The Algonquin scrupulously gathered up many kinds, and either threw them in the water, or burned them in the fire.

A single quotation from the Relation of 1634 will illustrate this. The missionary said:

The savages do not throw the bones of the beaver to the dogs, or of female porcupines, at least certain special bones; in short they very carefully take pains that the dogs shall eat no bone of birds or other animals which are taken in a snare. Otherwise they will take no more except with the greatest difficulty; besides there are within a thousand observations, for it is important only that the vertebrae or the rump alone should be given to these dogs, the rest must be thrown into the fire; still, for a beaver taken in a snare it is better to throw his bones into a river; it is a strange thing that they gather and pick up these things, and preserve them with so much care that you would say their hunt had been lost had they gone contrary to their superstitions. As I ridiculed them and told them that the beavers did not know what was done with their bones, they replied to me: You do not know how to take beavers, and you wish to talk about them; before the beaver is entirely dead, they said to me, his soul comes around by the cabin of the one who killed him, and notices carefully what they do with his bones; that if one gave them to the dogs the other beavers would be warned of it; that is why they would render themselves hard to catch: but they are very glad if they throw their bones into the fire or into a river, the snare especially, which has taken them, is well pleased. I told them that the Iroquois, as is done among us, threw the bones of the beaver to the dogs, and yet they very often took some, and that our French, beyond comparison, were accustomed to take more game than they, and yet our dogs were accustomed to eat the bones.

The Algonquins, of that day, extended this rule to fish, and it may have had wider applications still. To leave no permanent memorial it was necessary only to care for the bones on the lodge site. Outside of the circle they would soon perish, and this superstition prevented their casting them there. These lodges had no dumping places;

everything was disposed of on the spot.

In referring these mounds to the Algonquin family another fact is explained. These nations may not have been without earthenware, and perhaps most of them were not, in a limited way, but it was not so common as with the Iroquois and others. They were nomadic, and the lightest vessel possible suited them best. It was particularly necessary to have one not easily broken, and that could be readily replaced on a journey. Toward and north of the St. Lawrence the canoe birch abounded, and of this material their cooking vessels were formed. Their cooking was not very thorough, and hot stones, dropped into the water, heated it enough for their needs.

Why arrowheads are not found, nor other stone implements as a rule, is a more difficult question, but capable of various answers. There were careful aborigines, those who lost little, as well as those careless and wasteful. Articles were not so readily lost, but more readily found, in a cabin than in a village. The wooden arrow might have sufficed for most of the needs of the place. Some have suggested that the huts were those of a recent day, and that no purely Indian relics may be expected. I do not assent to this view, nor am I prepared to say with Mr. Marvin, that these forest men have left us traces of the oldest habitations in the State. The fact seems to be, however, that we must make these very modern, with but little to sustain this view, or place them before the Iroquois occupancy of New York and the St. Lawrence. Till the Iroquois sold their lands there has been no time within the last 300 years when it would have been safe for Algonquins to have habitations on Perch Lake. For a century before that, at least, Jefferson County was occupied by the Iroquoian family, and they had no wish for intruders. How much these mounds antedate the last four centuries is a harder problem. I think they may safely be placed within the past 500 years. Traditionally the Algonquin and Iroquois family arrived here nearly together, and at no remote period. An examination of the sites of their camps and towns seems to substantiate this, and these mounds suggest a period antedating that of their inveterate hostility. They were undefended, long used, and yet were in a territory claimed and held by the Iroquois for hundreds of years.

Two maps of the vicinity are given; one from a large county map, and the other from the public topographic survey, conspicuously differing in some respects. In the latter, plate 3, the lake is much shorter than in the former, and streams which enter the river in one flow into the lake in the other. The difference may be accounted for by the fact that part of the swampy shores were once included in the lake, when the water supply was greater. On the former map the general range of the mounds is indicated by the usual sign.

Other New York Mounds

A few supplementary remarks may be made on other mounds in New York, the larger part of the State having none, and most of those found being of small size and simple character. In some cases natural formations have been mistaken for these, having been used for burial or camps. In 27 counties some form of mound has been reported and a summary of these follows. They are most frequent west of the center of the State, and will be mentioned by counties.

Several occurred in Allegany County, and thence westward they were frequent. In the town of Conewango, Cattaraugus County, was a tumulus 13 feet high, with a diameter of 61 by 65 feet. Skeletons were found with relics. In the village of Randolph was a burial mound 10 feet high and 35 feet in diameter. In the town of Bucktooth, north side of the Allegheny, was a burial mound, 39 feet in diameter and 10 feet high. Another was in the town of Napoli, on Cold Spring Creek, which was 120 feet around. At Olean were several of these, one being 40 by 60 feet in diameter and nearly 10 feet high. One in Dayton was of the same height, and 120 feet in circumference. Another was on the west side of the Allegheny River, in the town of Cold Spring. This has been reported as 200 feet around and 20 feet high; probably an exaggeration. On Cold Spring Creek, 2 miles from the Allegheny, were two burial mounds, 10 feet high and 100 feet around. Others were in the towns of Leon and Conewango, in one of which were 8 sitting skeletons.

Quite a number were in Chautauqua County. One at Cassadaga Lake was 7 feet high and 30 feet in diameter. A stone mound near a fort in Ellington was 4 feet wide and 5 feet high. Two mounds near Griffith's point, Chautauqua Lake, were once 12 feet high and 40 feet in diameter. A number of similar mounds have been reported on both shores, and two near Jamestown. Another, near Rutledge, was 20 feet in diameter and 6 feet high. One in the village of Fredonia was 7 feet high. Another at Fluvanna seems recent. Most mounds west of Cayuga Lake were sepulchral.

Near Spring Lake, in Cayuga County, were small mounds with human remains, but these may have been incidental, as in some other places. On the high land of Howland Island, near the river, are one or two suggestive of Perch Lake. One is not very distinct, but the other stands out plainly. It is a circle with a diameter of 37 feet and an elevation of 30 inches, inclosing burnt earth and stone, but yielding no relics. The earth is in its natural condition for a considerable distance around. Some pits within the circle may be the work of explorers. This I examined July 18, 1902.

The noted burial mound in Greene, Chenango County, was 40 feet in diameter and 6 feet high. Several hut rings have been reported along the Chenango River, similar to those at Perch Lake, but those at Indian brook, a little south of Greene, prove to be caches.

Columbia and Schoharie Counties both had the stone heaps to which Indians added stones in passing.

Erie County had its full share of mounds. One at the mouth of Cattaraugus Creek was used for burial, but was probably natural. It was 50 feet across and from 10 to 15 feet high. The relics were modern.

There were several burial mounds on the east side of Cattaraugus Creek, two of which were excavated by Dr. A. L. Benedict of Buffalo, in 1900. As good accounts of such work by competent observers are rare in New York, his plans are given in plate 11 and his report is summarized from the *American Antiquarian* for 1901, p.99-107.

No. 1, a truncated mound in an open field when I saw it, is a mile north of the creek, and 600 feet north of the high bank of the ancient valley. It is nearly circular and about 70 feet in diameter. The central height is 4 feet, 8 inches, but he thought it was originally 10 or 11 feet high. It was made of sand loam, and there were depressions north and south in the general level of the field. It had been disturbed. At A were animal bones, ashes and charcoal at 3 feet, 5 inches from the surface; also bones of the aboriginal dog. At B was a heap of flat pieces of Hamilton slates, some of them waterworn. A rib and sacrum under these he thought those of the musk ox. At C was a fragmentary human skull, with other human bones, at a depth of 3 feet. Near this were flint arrows and knife, flint chips occurring elsewhere in the mound. Dr. Benedict's plans have the top to the south.

No. 2 resembles the last and has been reduced by plowing. It is quite near the creek, and a central shaft was sunk below the original soil in 1875 by William C. Bryant of Buffalo. Gravel was found 4 feet below the level at A by Dr. Benedict, and this occurred at 4 feet, 9 inches at H. At F was an oblong fireplace of waterworn stones. Between the top stone and one on the west side of the enclosure part of a pottery rim was found. There were small sherds at H. In the ashes under the top stone were calcined bones. A human astragalus was found at B, 4 feet southwest of the central stake, at a depth of 1 foot, 9 inches, covered with several round stones, 6 inches to a foot in diameter and an inch thick. A calcined long bone was found 15 feet south of the stake, which seemed part of a human tibia. At 7 feet, 10 inches south from the stake the bottom of the mound was of burnt clay and gravel, about 6 inches thick. Below this was a hollow space, beginning 3 feet, 7 inches from the surface of the mound. This was 9 or 10 inches deep, and extended every way 2 or 3 feet. The floor of this was of coarse gravel, about the size of hickory nuts, blackened, but showing no disturbance. Charred wood was occasionally found, some of considerable size. There were also small bits of mica. These seem hardly true burial mounds, though containing human bones.

Other mounds have been reported in Erie County 15 to 16 feet high and from 45 to 54 feet in diameter. One near the Indian fort at Buffalo was 5 or 6 feet high, and from 35 to 40 feet across. It is probable that Dr. Benedict's diameters may be too great, allowance not being made for increase at the base by washing down from above.

On St. Regis Island, Franklin County, was a mound 8 feet high, and another opposite, on the east bank of St. Regis River. Burial mounds were frequent along the St. Lawrence.

Small mounds have been reported on Tonawanda Creek, in Genesee County, but they may not have been artificial, though used for sepulture. The mound at the Bone fort, near Caryville, was 6 feet high and 30 feet wide, almost entirely composed of bones.

Two small mounds have been reported in Jefferson County, and many hut rings on the east hank of Black River, Lewis County, opposite the Deer River station. These are like those at Perch Lake.

In the summer of 1903 an early and notable ossuary was discovered by Mrs. R. D. Loveland of Watertown, near the long carrying place at the head of Chauniont Bay. A curious depression arrested her attention, and a little digging brought to light a human skull. She then turned over the search to others, who unfortunately had not her knowledge and skill, and no clear description is available from them. Dr. R. W. Amidon afterward visited the place, saw the relics, and obtained what information he could. Its importance comes from its age, the relics being mostly of early types. The pit is near and below the end of a ledge of Trenton limestone. At least 8 skeletons of vigorous adults were unearthed, from 2 to 4 feet below the surface, and mostly covered with boulders and flat stones. Two skulls were fractured, as though by a war club. A perfect clay vessel was destroyed by the diggers, but it was of a frequent form. A bird amulet, of green striped slate, was found. This was 5 1/2 inches long, rather broad, and with the head and tail almost on a plane with the body. There was also a bar amulet of sandstone, 6 inches long, and a perfect soapstone pipe of a frequent form. A flat bone bead, bone and horn implements, flint arrowheads or knives, were among other articles. This ossuary thus gives us some idea of what other things were used by those who had these amulets.

In Livingston County there was once a mound in the road from Dansville to Groveland, which was 4 or 5 feet high and 30 feet in diameter. Another was midway between Dansville and Scottsburg. A burial mound was 2 1/2 miles southeast of the head of Hemlock Lake. One at Mt. Morris was used for recent sepulture, but may not have been artificial, as it is said to have been 100 feet across and 8 to 10 feet high. Some accounts make the relics of early types, and it is probable it was used at various periods. On the Genesee River, near the Wheatland line, was a burial mound 8 feet high. Two mounds are also on the Wadsworth farm near Genesee. One is 3 feet high, but not quite 25 feet across; the other is much smaller. Both have been reduced in size. A stone heap at Lima traditionally had a

Plate 8 A fine mound on the Timmerman farm, at the base of a hill. Partly excavated in 1901. This is 33 feet wide and about 5 feet high. There are but few trees near this and it is a prominent object.

memorial character.

In Madison County, on Oneida Lake, are supposed Indian mounds, which are probably natural formations.

There was a mound in Monroe County, a few miles northwest of Scottsville. Two small mounds were west of Irondequoit Bay, on high land, the largest being less than 5 feet high. A large one was east of the bay, and another, east of the village of Penfield, was originally 40 feet in diameter and 8 or 9 feet high. Two burial mounds were on the east bank of Genesee River, half a mile below the lower fall. They were 4 feet high and 20 to 25 feet wide. There were other mounds in that vicinity. In Pittsford was a pile of large limestone boulders, the heap being about 12 feet square. Between Irondequoit landing and the lake was a cemetery of 200 small grave mounds, arranged in rows. The further character was not reported, but single graves are usually depressed. A mound was on the bluff south of Dunbar hollow, which contained stone implements. Mr. Harris thought a

Plate 9 Mound near the ruined La Farge mansion. Another joins it at the base. It is not one of the largest sizes, but it is on open ground on a lower terrace than the house and stands out prominently against the background of the lake. This mound has an extreme width of 34 feet.

small island on the west side of Irondequoit Bay was mostly artificial, as proved by excavations and grading. It was 90 feet long, 32 wide and 17 feet high, but was not sepulchral, though it contained many fine articles at a depth of 15 feet.

A mound described in Cambria, Niagara County, should be called an ossuary and contained metallic articles. A stone mound has been reported a mile west of Lockport, and an ordinary one at Gasport. Two burial mounds of large size were on Tonawanda Island. Another was in Wilson, and two in the town of Lewiston. In September 1903, the one marked D on Schoolcraft's map was opened. He called it "a small mound or barrow," but if it ever had much elevation cultivation had long before removed all signs of this. As it has not before been described a brief account of it will be given here. The first skull was found 6 or 8 inches below the present level of the ground, and the skeletons were estimated at over 300. Over 200 skulls were secured and none had been injured, the place representing well the ossuaries of Canada. The date may have been not far from 1620, perhaps a little later, while the Neutral nation still occupied land in New York. The pit, excavated by Mr. John Mackay of Niagara Falls, was about 18 feet long and from 12 to 14 feet wide, with a depth of 3 1/2 feet from the surface. The form was an irregular ellipse, and the bottom was of rock and clay. To make more room the pit had been widened about 18 inches from the bottom, and the smaller bones were placed in this addition. There were no traces of any lining to the pit, nor any suggestions of Jesuit contact, while earlier articles of European trade had reached the spot, possibly from the Dutch through the Five Nations. There were 24 iron axes, several brass kettles, 3 sword blades, 24 large and curious brass rings, 5 cylindric brass or copper beads, with other ornaments of shell. Through the kindness of Mr. Mackay I examined a number of these. The rings are simply short brass cylinders, bent in circles, and the beads are long brass tubes, precisely like those occurring in the Mohawk valley. One of these is 11 inches long and 5/8 inch in diameter. Mr. Mackay has an interesting collection, well repaying study.

Some burial mounds have been reported in New York City, apparently natural elevations used for sepulture.

Some supposed mounds in Oneida County are also of doubtful character, nothing having been determined by examination.

In Onondaga County, near Baldwinsville, were two large stone heaps, covering human bones, and two burial mounds were on the west side of Onondaga outlet. One was circular and stood out prominently from the bank behind it. The other was oblong, being 12 feet long and 3 feet high when I sketched it, and had then been somewhat reduced.

At the modern Seneca castle near Geneva, where Johnson built a fort in 1756, is an artificial mound about 6 feet high and used as a cemetery. It is probably rather graded than built up. There was a small recent mound at Clifton Springs.

In Carlton, Orleans County, on the north bank of Oak Orchard Creek, is a small oblong mound, 20 by 30 feet in diameter. Another small mound was 30 rods away.

Bone Hill, at Oswego Falls, was a place of sepulture, now known to be of natural formation. It was 6 rods in diameter and 40 feet high, and has been removed.

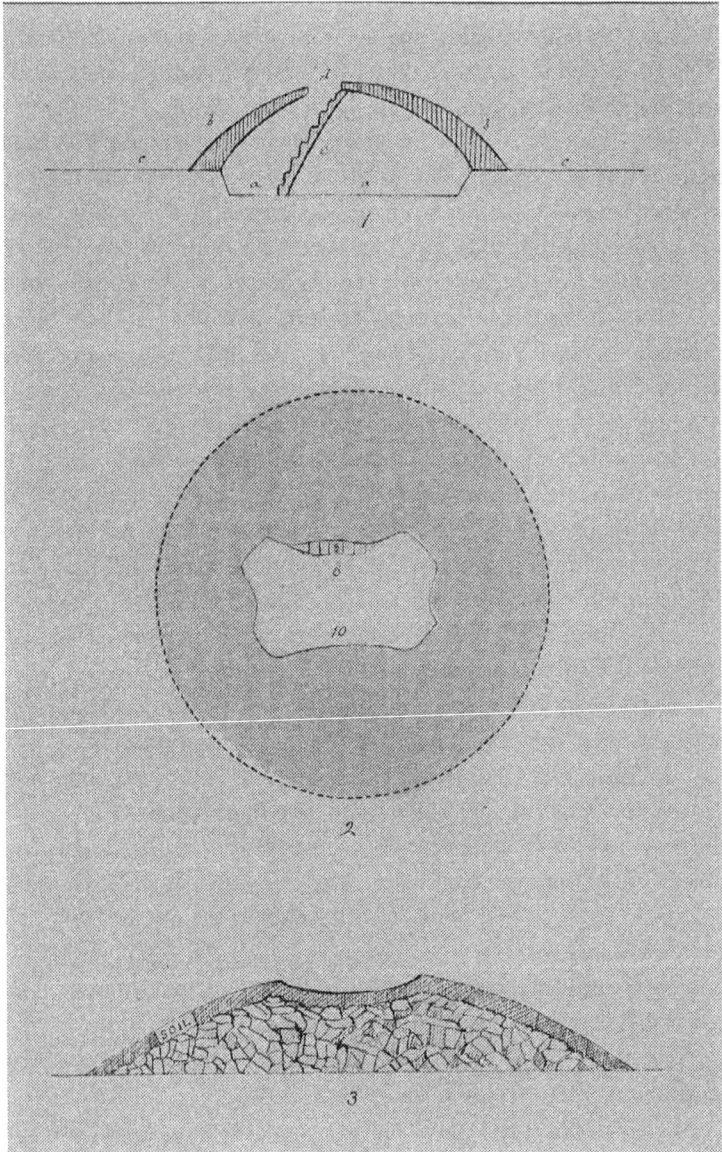

Plate 10 Figure 1 is a sketch, furnished by Harlan I. Smith, being a section of an earth hut of the Thompson River Indians, showing how mounds of this kind are sometimes formed. Figure 2 is a plan of a mound on the Bay of Quinté, on the north shore of Lake Ontario, and showing a central excavation. Figure 3: Section of a mound at the same place, showing the interior filled with stones, the covering of soil, and the central depression.

In Unadilla was a supposed Indian monument, 20 feet in diameter, 10 feet high, and of a conical form. There was a mound at Oneonta, and a supposed burial mound at Cooperstown.

In Tioga County there was a circular burial mound at Owego. Several mounds were in the vicinity of Newark Valley. One of these was 15 feet high and 250 feet around, suggesting natural formation.

In Wayne County I examined several mounds July 18, 1902. One was northwest of Savannah and in the midst of camp sites. It is circular and but slightly separated from the ridge behind. It is 60 feet across and 3 feet high. Another burial mound north of Crusoe Creek and northeast of this, is now small and low, but distinct. Another was examined 2 1/2 miles south of Savannah. It is at the south end of a ridge containing caches, from which it has been separated by excavation. The bodies were apparently laid on the surface and the earth heaped upon them. It is 30 feet across and about 7 feet high. The first of these mounds shows little work.

In Wyoming County is a burial mound about 4 miles south of Portage.

In Yates County a small burial mound on Bluff point is 9 feet long and 4 feet high.

These are all the burial or monumental mounds thus far reported in New York, as distinguished from defensive earthworks. Very few indeed resemble those of Perch Lake, and this led to the special examination of the latter. Their peculiar character is emphasized by this comparison with New York mounds elsewhere, and though scattered examples may yet be found here, it is quite probable that nowhere else in the State will they be seen in such numbers or in such fine preservation. They form a unique group, well worthy of further study, though offering little in the way of fine relics, or indeed of any at all.

By way of caution it should be remarked that the height of mounds is commonly made too great unless accurately determined; and there is also a disposition to consider any symmetric elevation of moderate size an Indian mound. Even when human bones are found in them they are not always artificial.

A curious spot 1 1/2 miles west-southwest of Unadilla may be described here, having never been mentioned before. For the account

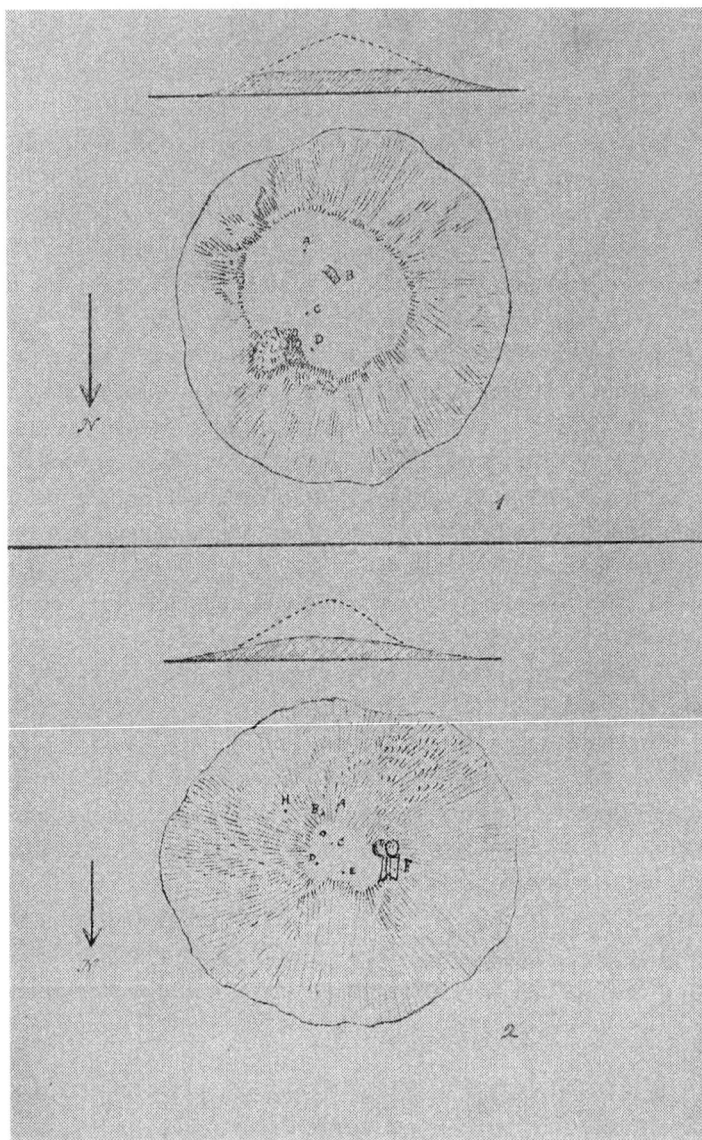

Plate 11   Figure 1: Truncated mound excavated by Dr. A.L. Benedict in 1900, on the east side of Cattarangus Creek, N.Y. The upper figure is of the recent condition and probable original form. The plan shows the position of various points of interest reached in excavating. At A were animal bones; at B pieces of Hamilton slate; at C human bones. Mound diameter is 70 feet. Figure 2: A mound near the same creek and much like the last. At A and H, gravel was found; at F a stone fireplace; at B were human bones. There was also charred wood.

and chart, thanks are due to Mr. Harry B. Cecil of that place. It is on the farm of Enoch H. Copley and in a woodland of about 33 acres, the whole of which is a series of moraines and kettle-shaped hollows. In the largest of these hollows is a shallow pond, marked A in the diagram, plate 12, figure 1. The shaded part B has been partly filled in for the Delaware & Hudson Railroad. The pond is surrounded by moraines, C C C, about 100 feet high, and a road D, follows the north and east margins. At E, F, G, are rude stone walls from 2 to 4 feet high. Mr. Cecil said:

> At one time I supposed these had been constructed to get rid of the rocks that were in the way, but this could not be the case, as the stones could have been dumped into the pond very much more easily, and it would have materially helped to widen the road D. The oldest residents say that these piles and walls have always been there. At H, until a short time ago, were two circles made of rocks loosely thrown together. They measured 10 feet across and were contiguous, having openings at the remote parts of their circumferences. I turned these over carefully, but failed to find anything of Indian workmanship and the soil beneath was apparently undisturbed. At I was another stone wall. At J is a heap of undisturbed rocks. At K is a carefully made road, about 8 feet wide and extending about 300 feet in a westerly direction, gradually ascending to 50 feet above the pond level. No explanation can be given of this unless it was part of a trail. Below this road and above the wall at E, is a stone heap, and above the road is a large hollow filled up with stones of all descriptions. I am positive that these heaps are not natural. All these remains are included in about half an acre.

This account is free from extravagance and suggests the use of the spot as a pound for deer, terminating a driveway. These and other animals would naturally resort there to drink. With or without contracting hedges they would follow their own paths, and

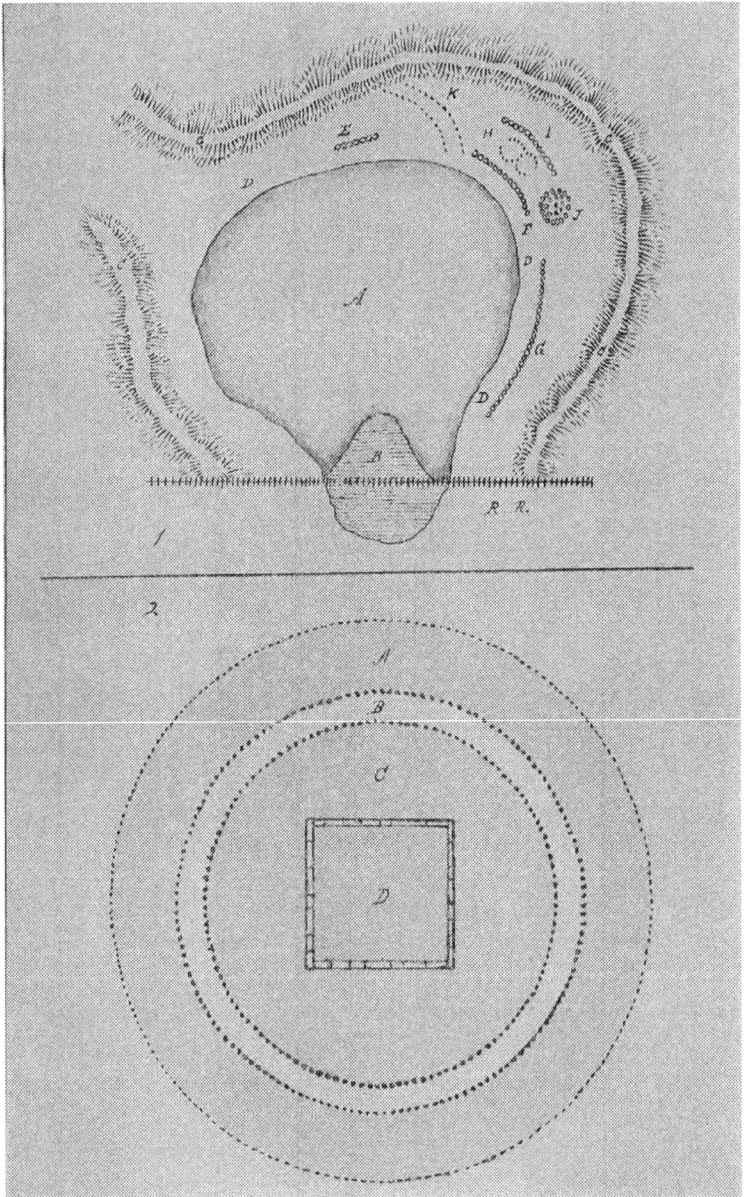

Plate 12 Figure 1: *Supposed deer pound by a pond near Unadilla. A is the pond; C moraines; D a round around the pond; E, F, G, I are stone walls; H stone circles; K is a graded way. Figure 2: Plan of Perch Lake mound. A is the outer slope; B the crown of the ridge; C the inner slope; D the rectangular stone fireplace in the center. This is the ground plan of the mound shown on plate 4.*

the roadway would turn them toward the double walls, I, F, when driven. Some would escape only to encounter other hunters at the wall G. In the press others might turn back and meet hunters at the wall E. The circles may have been the foundations of hunting lodges, and the season of wild fowl would afford a secondary use. The usual course was to make a pound of stakes and branches, but the primitive hunter was quick to avail himself of natural advantages, and was not sparing of work.

Excavations of the Perch Lake mounds were performed in 1968 by New York archeologist William A. Ritchie and again in 2002 by archeologists Jack and Diane Coates and Juliann Van Nest. Ritchie's excavation provided radiocarbon dates on three samples, yielding dates of 930 A.D. ± 80 years, 140 B.C. ± 100 years, and 630 A.D. ± 60 years. The 2002 excavation produced a second set of radiocarbon dates: 470 A.D. ± 70 years, 620 ± 70 years, 1830 ± 70 years, and 2020 ± 30 years.

Three primary, but not mutually exclusive, hypotheses have been put forward to explain the function of the Perch Lake Mounds since they were first discovered.

The first is that the mounds were used primarily for ritual. Franklin B. Hough speculated in the mid-1800s that the mounds were collapsed burial vaults, others suggested that they were crematoria. However, no human remains have been found in any of the mounds. Other possible ritual uses, proposed by Ritchie, is that the mounds were an expression of new fire ceremonialism, in which fire was revered as the embodiment of a supreme deity.

The second hypothesis is that the mounds were lodges with perishable superstructures. Beauchamp believed that the mounds could be "hut rings," marking permanent dwellings, like those found in California. The current evidence does not support this conclusion, however. Beauchamp also thought they might be seasonal lodges, a form of earth-banked conical wood lodge. Ritchie later speculated they might be sweat lodges.

The third possibility is that the mounds served an economic purpose and were actually processing facilities of some kind, perhaps of fish, mammals, shellfish, or plants.

Based on current information, most of these hypotheses cannot be rejected. It's also possible, though only marginally so, that the mounds served more than one function. More likely, the mounds served some purpose that has yet to be deciphered.

WILLIAM MARTIN BEAUCHAMP (1830-1925) was an archaeologist, historian, and Episcopalian minister. Born in Coldenham, Orange County, New York, Beauchamp attended Skaneateles Academy and the Delancey Divinity School in Geneva, New York. He was ordained in the priesthood of the Episcopalian Church in 1863. After retiring in 1900, he devoted much of his time to research and writing on the Iroquois. He was one of the great authorities on the history and institutions of the Iroquois.